FUSS-FREE
VEGAN

FUSS-FREE VEGAN

101

Everyday Comfort Food Favorites, Veganized

Sam Turnbull

appetite
by RANDOM HOUSE

Appetite by Random House® and colophon are registered trademarks of Penguin Random House LLC.

Library and Archives Canada Cataloguing in Publication is available upon request.
ISBN: 978-0-14-753035-6
eBook ISBN: 978-0-14-753036-3

Book design by Lisa Jager

Printed and bound in China

Published in Canada by Appetite by Random House®,
a division of Penguin Random House Canada Limited.

www.penguinrandomhouse.ca

10 9 8 7 6 5 4 3 2 1

This book is dedicated to my mom & dad, who have supported and encouraged me through all my craziness
(which I proudly get from them).

TABLE of CONTENTS

THE RECIPES

FEAST YOUR EYES & BELLY

SWEET TOOTH

VEGAN STAPLES

HELLO!

You might be surprised to hear that the moment I decided I was going to go vegan, I was completely and utterly bummed about it.

Let me explain. I NEVER — not in a million and six years — thought I would become vegan.

I grew up in a household where there was a flock of chickens (both for eggs and for eating), the freezers were stocked full of meat, steaks were cooked rare, and there were even real animal heads decorating the walls (not that I ever liked the heads). Doesn't that just sound like the most vegan household you have ever heard of? I'm sure you can imagine that switching to veganism was a BIG change for me.

As a kid I always loved animals. I had dogs, cats, gerbils, turtles, and even a rabbit named Gravy (no, I didn't realize how incredibly odd that was at the time). But even though I loved animals, I was still an avid meat eater. This lifestyle made sense to me: animals were killed because we "needed" to eat meat and that seemed a-ok to me.

I thought vegetarians, and especially vegans, were extreme and silly. They were for sure all dying of protein deficiency. (Insert eye roll here.) So, that's how I was coasting along through life. Loving my pets, being creeped out by fur and taxidermy, all while wearing leather and eating meat, eggs, and dairy.

So how did a proud meat eater like me switch overnight to never touching a piece of meat again? Well, one fine day in 2012, I made what turned out to be the best decision ever: to sit down and watch a documentary about being vegan. That doc triggered some uncomfortable questions in my brain, so I followed that up with every health, environment, and animal cruelty book and film I could get my hands on.

The result? You guessed it, here I am today, *dun dun duuuuun!* A vegan. (Hi!)

By the end of my documentary and book binge-fest, two things were absolutely clear to me:

1. I was officially going vegan.

2. I didn't want to be vegan.

After all of my research, it made 100% logical sense to me to be vegan. It was better for my health, the environment, and, of course, the animals. The problem was, I actually hated the idea of adopting a vegan lifestyle. I almost wished I could un-learn all of the facts I had learned. I loved eating meat and cheese, and I really didn't want to be known as "that weird vegan girl." Well, I couldn't un-learn, so I had to come up with a new plan of attack: be the best damn vegan I knew how to be!

Having grown up in a family of chefs, foodies, butchers, and hunters (yep, it's true), I wasn't surprised that they were not super excited to hear of my new food direction. There were jokes and teasing. Everyone thought it was some new diet trend, that I would likely start eating meat again soon, and just like everyone I met, they thought my food would be boring and probably weird. I wanted to prove everyone wrong.

I had always loved to cook, so I started researching vegan cooking. I stocked my cupboards with what the recipes required: hard-to-find, expensive, and odd ingredients such as arrowroot starch, brown rice syrup, xylitol, guar gum, spelt, hemp, and other weird things that I still have lingering in some back corner. All the recipes had names that included the words "energy," "glow," "detox," or "power," and were mainly for bars, balls, juices, smoothies, and salads. They required hours of prep, dehydrating, straining, and had a ton of steps. Cookies were raw, chocolate was frozen, desserts were healthy, dinner was spiralized, grain bowls were a must, and everything had kale, quinoa, chia seeds, sprouts, avocado, and coconut oil in it. This to me was indeed boring and weird food.

Now, don't get me wrong, there is nothing wrong with those kind of recipes. They just weren't for me. Sometimes I love sipping a smoothie or a juice, but for the most part I just want good ol' pancakes or a big bowl of pasta. Why did I have to become all sprouts and kale just because I was vegan?

I began playing around in the kitchen, I stopped the costly trips to the health food stores, and instead of using the weird recipes I had found online, I started being inspired by my old favorite recipes. I learned that juices weren't required, I didn't have to love energy balls, and I could make meals that actually appealed to me, my friends, and my family (whether they were vegan or not). I soon discovered that *any meal* could be made vegan, and with a few clever tweaks, a large spice cabinet, and a dash of creativity, I began loving my recipes. In fact, *I loved them more than the original animal product-based recipes.*

Not only were my new creations satisfying, hearty, full of flavor, and straight-up delicious, but they were just as easy to make as any other meal. With limitation came inspiration, and before I knew it, going vegan had become one of the best decisions I'd ever made!

As a sweet bonus, I saw my health improve. I didn't even know that I had been feeling bad until I learned what it felt like to feel great! Gone were the days of feeling bloated after eating, of having a sensitive stomach, of getting drowsy mid-afternoon, of unbuttoning my jeans after meals, and of feeling guilty and grossed out when I thought about what my dinner really was. I was now healthier, leaner, more energetic, and just overall happier. *The best, and most surprising part of going vegan was that I absolutely loved it!*

I began documenting my recipes so I could make them again and again. At first I was just taking quick snaps on my phone and jotting down the ingredients, but I decided a better plan was to (not so subtly) woo my friends, family, and anyone who would listen to the greener side by sharing my recipes online. And so my blog, *It Doesn't Taste Like Chicken*, was born. Hot dang, it worked! Friends, family, vegans, vegetarians, and omnivores from across the world were making my recipes — and raving about them!

I think I'm like a dog. Pat me on the head and tell me I'm good and I will love you forever. As the feedback started rolling in, I really grew passionate about sharing my recipes. Not only that, but I was helping to show people that a plant-based diet can be totally delicious, easy, doable, good for you, and not at all weird!

I'm so proud to say that this is the cookbook I wish I had when I went vegan. All of my approachable, comfort food favorites, and everyday meals, made vegan. No fussing about, just good ol' food that everyone will love, vegan or not. **Bonus points:** These recipes are all a little healthier than the original animal product versions! Photos galore, easy step-by-step instructions, and totally and utterly delicious food. These are my fuss-free vegan favorites.

I hope you love these recipes as much
as I have loved creating (and devouring) them.

Bon Appetegan,

Sam Turnbull

What You WON'T Find in this Cookbook

➡ **Fake, mock, or "un" recipes.** A common trend in vegan cooking is to use fake meats, or name recipes "unchicken" or "mock-tuna." That's all fine, but I don't eat fake food. I eat real food. Throughout the book I have recipes for things like carrot *lox*, tofu *bolognese*, and various *cheese* recipes. I'm claiming the words not as parts of animals, but as dish and flavor descriptions. I don't think there is any problem with recreating familiar tastes and textures, but I call it what it is, and not what it isn't. The term "veggie burger," for example, was coined in the early '80s, but before then, all burgers had to be made from meat. I'm doing the same thing with the recipes in this book: progressing the food vocabulary. Even the word "meat" isn't exclusive to animal; it simply means food that is solid versus what is liquid—that's why we call it coconut meat, or nut meat. I'm not eating chicken and I don't want to pretend I am, but eating coconut bacon? Yus, puh-lease!

➡ **Fancy-schmancy, bizarre, hard-to-pronounce, difficult-to-find ingredients.** I will introduce you to a few of my favorite ingredients, such as nutritional yeast (obsessed!), chia seeds, and miso paste. These ingredients, along with all of the others I use, can usually be found in your local grocery store.

➡ **Weird, bland, or scary-looking food!** Yes, my recipes are vegan, but I swear you'll barely notice.

What You WILL Find in this Cookbook

➡ **Hearty, and satisfying comfort food recipes.** These are simple, scrumptious meals for everyone, vegan or not. You'll find pastas, burgers, burritos, soups, cookies, cupcakes, and all things delicious and familiar.

➡ **Quick and easy recipes that will fit right into your day-to-day life.** Many of these recipes can be whipped up without stress—even after a long day.

➡ **Trustworthy recipes.** My friends and family were happy to chow down, and they've helped me test my recipes over and over again, so I know these dishes will turn out perfectly every time.

MY VEGAN KITCHEN

Whether you were raised vegan or you're completely new to this lifestyle, having a few basics in your kitchen is the key to making vegan cooking a breeze. A great way to start this new way of eating without the stress is to simply surround yourself with vegan food. If you have an entirely vegan kitchen, you don't even have to think about it when you eat, because every option you have is already vegan. Simple.

If you are just making the switch to veganism, first of all, congrats and a big warm welcome from me! You may currently have a kitchen stocked with animal products. It's up to you whether you gradually make the switch to veganism or jump right in all at once, like I did. Whatever approach you choose, this list will help you set up a go-to vegan kitchen. You probably already have a lot of these ingredients in your kitchen, so it shouldn't be leaps and bounds from what you're used to.

A FUSS-FREE VEGAN PANTRY

Beans, Beans, the Magical Fruit

Canned or dried, beans are super nutritious, filling, and can bulk up a meal in no time, so I always have them on hand. Canned beans are the quickest when life is a little busy (which is almost always), so I usually buy chickpeas, black beans, kidney beans, and refried beans this way. I generally buy red, green, and brown lentils dry because they're so quick to cook.

Cool Tip
To make beans less . . . er . . . musical, make sure you rinse them really well before you use them.

Grains & Breads

Carbs are good for you, especially when they're whole grain. My go-to's are brown or white rice, plain bread crumbs, panko bread crumbs, sandwich bread, hamburger and hot dog buns, soft tortillas, and puff pastry (for my lentil loaf). Most bread is vegan, but check the ingredients to be sure.

Pasta & Noodles

Most store-bought dried pasta and noodles are vegan (woot woot!), but double-check the ingredients to be sure. I always try to have a variety of shapes and sizes in my pantry. In this book I use rice noodles (wide and spaghetti shape), macaroni, fettuccini, linguini, spaghetti, and lasagna noodles. If you are gluten-free or want to eat more whole grains (always a good idea), brown rice pasta is a good option.

Nut Butters

I mean, can you ever go wrong with peanut butter? Nope. (Well, unless you're allergic, of course . . .) I call for it in several recipes in this book, but if you prefer you can sub almond butter, cashew butter, or any other nut butter you like in those recipes. I always use natural peanut butter, so look for ones that contain just nuts and maybe salt, but no added sugar or oils.

Cool Tip
When you bring natural nut butter home, store it upside down until you're ready to use it. The oil will rise to the bottom of the jar, making it much easier to stir when you open it.

Cashews & Other Nuts

You'll notice that I use raw cashews a lot throughout this book, and that's because they are magical and add glorious creaminess to any recipe. So buy them in bulk when they are on sale. If you can't eat cashews, try macadamia nuts or blanched almonds. The result won't be exactly the same, but it will still be scrumptious. I like to soften the cashews so they can easily be blended (see more about this on page 13). Other nuts I call for in recipes are walnuts and peanuts. Add those to your shopping list, too.

Seeds

I use either ground chia seeds or ground flax seeds as binders in my veggie burgers, bean balls, and lentil loaf. These days my go-to is ground chia seeds (I prefer white) because when you mix them with water, they thicken instantly. Flax seeds take about 10 minutes to thicken, but work just as well. You can buy chia seeds ground, but buy flax seeds whole and then grind them yourself using a coffee grinder or high-speed blender. I've found that pre-ground flax is often rancid and dried out. I also use white or black (or both) sesame seeds to garnish some dishes.

Non-Dairy Milks

I'm a big fan of plant-based milks like soy, almond, and cashew, but there are even more options to choose from, such as rice milk, hemp milk, oat milk, coconut milk . . . the list goes on. Some non-dairy milks can be found in the refrigerated section of the grocery store, but there is usually an even larger variety found in the aisles, in shelf-stable cartons. Every brand has a different taste, so test a few out until you find your favorite, or try making your own (I have a great recipe on my blog!). I find that unsweetened soy milk is the best option when it comes to baking, but if it's not your thing, almond is a great alternative.

Whenever I call for a non-dairy milk in my recipes, I'm always referring to the plain unsweetened version—do not add vanilla, or chocolate-flavored milks to any dish unless specified, as it could totally ruin it. Many stores will also carry soy and almond creams intended for coffee.

Canned Coconut Milk & Coconut Cream

Full-fat coconut milk is a great way to add richness to a dish; just make sure you shake the can well before measuring. Note that different brands vary a lot in quality. For many of my recipes it doesn't matter too much what kind you use, but in my coconut whipped cream recipe (page 181) I call for coconut cream or premium coconut milk. The better-quality coconut milks will generally be more expensive, but you can always do the shake test: shake the can and listen. The less liquidy it sounds (i.e. the less noise), the thicker and richer the coconut milk is. I always keep several cans of coconut milk in my cupboard for making creamy sauces and baking, and I store a few cans of the extra-rich stuff in the back of my fridge so they're ready to go for coconut whipped cream.

Baking Ingredients

When it comes to baking, I like to keep it simple and stick to the basics that are readily available at every grocery store. Baking powder, baking soda, and vanilla extract are my three staples that I use throughout this book.

Herbs & Spices

Whenever someone tells me that vegan food is bland, I like to point out that their entire spice cabinet is vegan! Herbs and spices are an easy way to add flavor and interest to a dish. I've listed below all of the ones you will need to complete every recipe in this book. Some will be familiar to you; some may be new.

⇨ **Fresh Herbs & Spices:**
Basil, cilantro, garlic, ginger, green onions, hot peppers, jalapeños, mint.

⇨ **Dried Herbs & Spices:**
Black pepper, celery seed, chili powder, chives, cinnamon, dill, dry mustard, garlic powder, ground cloves, ground cumin, onion powder, oregano, parsley, pumpkin pie spice, red pepper flakes, salt, sweet and smoked paprika, thyme, turmeric, and whole star anise.

Black Salt

In some recipes I give the option of using black salt (also known as *kala namak*). The crazy thing about black salt is that it tastes just like eggs, so if you are someone who loves the taste of eggs, you might want to consider picking some up. Disappointingly, black salt isn't actually black, it's pink, but don't confuse it with Himalayan salt. That's a totally different thing. You can find black salt in Indian grocery stores or order it online.

Liquid Smoke

Liquid smoke is liquid gold when you are looking for a (dare I say) meaty flavor. It is the natural condensation collected from the smoke of a fire, and adding a small amount to your dish will give it a smoky BBQ flavor. Look for it right next to the BBQ sauces in your grocery store.

Vinegars & Citrus

Vinegars and citrus can add great flavors to dressings and sauces. I always have apple cider vinegar, balsamic vinegar, rice vinegar, lemons, and limes on hand. I also use apple cider vinegar or lemon juice in some of my baking to help cakes rise and get fluffy. (Don't worry, you can't taste it!)

Vegetable Broth

Vegetable broth is the easy substitute for chicken or beef broth. You can buy it in liquid form, or use the cubes or powder that you dissolve into water. All work just fine for the recipes in this book.

Cool Tip

Save leftover veggie scraps in your freezer (onions peels, carrot tops, herb stems, celery leaves, etc.) and when you have a big bag full, simmer the scraps in water for about 45 minutes. Strain out the veggies, and voila! You made a homemade vegetable broth using something you would otherwise throw away.

Oils

Olive oil, canola oil, coconut oil, and sesame oil are all staples in my kitchen. Canola oil is perfect for baking as it is flavorless and light, but you could also sub vegetable or safflower oil. Coconut oil has the unique quality of being solid at room temperature, which helps firm up some recipes, like the delicious cheese ball (page 62) in this book. You can also use coconut oil in place of vegan butter when it isn't available, but coconut oil doesn't provide the buttery flavor, so always opt for vegan butter when you can.

Nutritional Yeast

I get it. This is a TERRIBLY named food. It doesn't sound delicious at all. But it is, pinky swear! Nutritional yeast is a flaky yellow powder that doesn't have any rising properties like the yeast used in bread. It's used purely for flavor and is (you guessed it) nutritious. Vegans love it because it gives any dish a cheesy, nutty kind of taste. If you don't like it at first, I recommend you keep trying it. I thought it was weird the first time I had it, and now I sprinkle it all over popcorn as one of my favorite snacks. Cool vegans like to call it "nooch."

Miso Paste

Miso soup is an easy yummy snack, but I tend to use miso to help get those umami flavors in cheesy dishes. It comes in different colors, and my preference is the white version, which is lighter in both color and flavor than the darker kinds. You'll often find miso paste in the grocery aisles, then store it in the fridge after it's opened.

Sweeteners

Agave and pure maple syrup are great alternatives to honey. Good ol' white and brown sugar are perfect for baking, but some companies use bone char to whiten sugar, which will not be listed in the ingredients. Before you buy sugar, check the company website, or send them an email if the information isn't clear. If you're unsure, a safe bet is to buy organic, which is always bone char–free.

Flours & Starches

Whole wheat flour, all-purpose flour, gluten-free all-purpose flour blend, cornstarch, and tapioca starch (also known as tapioca flour) are all good to have on hand. If you're making my vegan cheeses, tapioca starch is an absolute must. It's what makes the cheeses melty and stretchy. Cornstarch is great for thickening sauces, as you will see in this book, but

won't get the same results as tapioca starch when making melty, stretchy vegan cheeses.

Cool Tip

You can make your own tapioca starch by grinding tapioca pearls into a powder in a coffee grinder or high-powered blender.

Chocolate

Chocolate is made from the cacao bean, so it's actually totally vegan until dairy is added to it. Having said that, most dark chocolate is vegan, but always check the ingredients to make sure. The health food section of your grocery store might carry vegan chocolate as well. I use chocolate chips in this book, and I find many brands are accidentally vegan!

A FUSS-FREE VEGAN FRIDGE & FREEZER

Fruit

Fresh and frozen fruit are great for snacks, making smoothies, and adding to oatmeal. I store most of my fruit at room temperature, while some berries and other fruits are kept in the fridge.

Cool Tip

Freeze peeled bananas solid, then blend them in a food processor with a splash of non-dairy milk to make totally guilt-free vegan soft serve ice cream! Add other frozen fruit, cocoa powder, vanilla extract, or cinnamon for different flavors. Boom!

Veggies

Did you know that there are around 20,000 edible plant species in the world, but the average American diet is mostly made up of only 20 of those!? And people think vegans are the boring ones! As a vegan, I now have a more varied diet than I ever did before.

Having said that, I call for pretty basic veggies throughout this book because I like my recipes to be easy and accessible. But don't be afraid to think outside the potato—there are so many delicious veggies to be had. Some less common veggies I love are puffball and hen of the wood mushrooms, black tomatoes, purple potatoes, watermelon radishes, lotus root, and broccoli rabe. I use heart of palm in a couple recipes in this book. Unlike some palm oil, most canned varieties of heart of palm are sustainable and come from farmed peach palms. But if you're looking for a substitute, try artichoke hearts. It's a different flavor, but it's a good substitution.

Tofu

I love me some tofu. Some people claim it's bland, and those people are right! Just like if you were to eat chicken, you would never eat it plain. It's all about what you do to the tofu to make it awesome. Tofu comes in different firmnesses, so pay attention to what type I call for in a recipe, as it will make a big difference to the outcome of the dish. I use extra-firm tofu when I want a chewier bite, but I use silken in sauces and in my vegan cheesecake for a lovely creaminess.

In the recipes where I call for tofu, you'll noticed that I sometimes specify "pressed." This refers to tofu that has had as much water as possible removed from it. To do this, lay tofu slices out on a clean tea towel and fold the edges of the towel over the slices to cover them. Then you press the tofu by putting a cutting board on top, and then something heavy on top of the cutting board, like a few cans of beans. Press for 15–30 minutes to squeeze out as much water as possible. (I also have a great tutorial on my blog!)

Cool Tip

You can freeze extra-firm tofu, then thaw it and squeeze the water out. This gives the tofu a completely different, almost spongy texture. Some people love it, some people hate it. It might be worth a try to see how you feel about it.

Tempeh

Tempeh is made from whole soybeans that are formed into a block and then fermented. It tastes bitter and nutty, and has a dense, crumbly texture. It can be more difficult to find than tofu, but if you come across it, you may want to try some to see if you enjoy it.

Cool Tip

Tempeh can have a bitter taste, but you can easily fix that if you steam it for about 10 minutes before cooking it.

Vegan Cheeses

More and more vegan cheeses are becoming available in stores. Some are great, others not so great. Beware of sneaky cheeses—soy cheeses sometimes contain milk. These are just intended to be lactose-free, not vegan, so read your labels. Personally, as you will see throughout this book, I prefer to make my own cheeses. It's less expensive, I know that they're 100% vegan, and they taste so very yummy!

Vegan Butter & Vegetable Shortening

Not all margarines are vegan, so make sure you check the ingredients. Vegetable shortening is vegan, but make sure you're not picking up lard! In many of these recipes I give the option to use either vegan butter or coconut oil. Vegan butter will always be the better option as it provides the right flavor, but when in a pinch or if vegan butter is difficult for you to find, feel free to use coconut oil.

Condiments

My cupboard and fridge are always stocked with these essentials: ketchup, soy sauce, hot sauce, mustard, relish, pickles, capers, olives, sauerkraut, tomato paste, marinated artichoke hearts, and sun-dried tomatoes. All of these are already vegan, so no need to stress. BBQ sauce sometimes contains honey, bacon, or fish, so watch out for that, but many brands are vegan. Or you can just make your own (page 209)! Vegan mayonnaise is becoming more popular, but you can always use my recipe on page 208 to make your own and save yourself some dollars.

MY GO-TO KITCHEN TOOLS

When it comes to kitchen tools, a vegan kitchen is really no different from a non-vegan kitchen. Well, ok, you probably aren't going to need a meat grinder, but you never know, it might come in handy one day!

The tools listed below are the ones that I find the most useful in my kitchen. While you can get by with a pretty simple kitchen, you might want to consider investing in these as they'll make your cooking life just so much easier. Some of my recipes require a blender or food processor, but I try to give options where I can, in case you don't have either.

Chef's Knife

My favorite kitchen tool is a good chef's knife. Don't bother buying a whole knife set—instead, invest your money in one good chef's knife about 8 inches long and with a wide blade. A chef's knife might look like a big scary knife, but it will make chopping a breeze. The size and weight of it will make it easier to cut veggies, and the wide blade can be used for crushing garlic or scooping up chopped veggies. Pick up a knife sharpener while you're at it, and use it. Remember that sharp knives are actually safer than dull knives because they are predictable—they cut the way you expect them to cut.

Blender

Any blender will do, but if you're looking to invest in a good one, I highly recommend getting a Blendtec (what I use) or a Vitamix. These high-powered machines make sauces perfectly smooth and super creamy, but they can also do things like grind flax or chia seeds. You can even skip soaking or boiling cashews in many recipes if they need to be blended because these blenders are strong enough to purée them unsoftened.

Food Processor

While blenders are great for liquids, you will want a food processor for chopping or blending thicker recipes where you might want some texture, such as with chickpea salad sandwiches (page 96) or veggie burger patties (page 93). My food processor has a big bowl and also a smaller bowl insert, making it perfect for large or small batches. I also love when they come with added blades for slicing and shredding—it can really speed up the prep time of a recipe.

VEGAN ON A BUDGET

I've got great news for you: a vegan diet is generally much less expensive than a non-vegan diet. Just take a gander at a non-vegan grocery bill and you'll see that meat and cheese are likely the most expensive items on the list! A can of beans will be less expensive than a steak any day. But, if your budget is tight, here are my tips for keeping the costs down.

Avoid Packaged Foods

You're paying for a bunch of people to prepare that recipe, package it, brand it, and market it to you. Not only that, but processed foods aren't as good for you as fresh food anyway, so stick to whole plant foods. You'll see throughout this book that I very rarely call for packaged goods, and I even have recipes to make your own staples such as BBQ sauce, mayonnaise, salad dressings, and pizza dough.

Buy in Season

Produce that's in season will not only taste better, it's also usually more affordable. Each year I get excited for cherry, peach, citrus, and strawberry season, because there is nothing better than snacking on fresh ripe fruit. If there are really good deals, you can freeze fruit to use later.

Buy in Bulk

Items like raw cashews can be crazy expensive in the grocery store, but hop over to a bulk food store and you can often get a way better deal. Items like cashews also store well, so stock up when they are on sale!

Visit Small Grocery Stores

I find that smaller grocery stores that are not part of a major chain often have super-good deals and fun finds. There is a little East Indian grocery store near my house that I frequent for coconut oil, nuts, rice, and some produce at almost half the price of my regular store.

Stick to the Basics

Beans, lentils, rice, and potatoes are all very filling, very nutritious, and very affordable. Toss in a little fresh produce and your body and taste buds will be totally satisfied.

Cook from Scratch, Freeze for Later

Luckily there is a whole book in your hands right now that will help you cook meals from scratch (or pretty darn close). Make larger batches of these recipes and freeze some for later. Soups are one of my favorite meals to freeze because they freeze so nicely. Just take a batch out of the freezer in the morning, pop it in the fridge to thaw, then heat it up when you get home and make some toast, for a perfect lazy weeknight meal.

HOW TO SOFTEN
Cashews
(or other nuts)

The idea of softening cashews may be new to you, but no worries, my friend, it's super-duper easy, and it'll change your vegan game. I realize you might be wondering why you would even want to soften nuts. I mean, soaking your nuts, pretty funny-sounding, right? Softening nuts makes them blendable. Raw cashews have this magic quality of being incredibly creamy when blended while not having much flavor, making them the perfect creamy base for sauces and cheeses.

There are two methods I recommend for softening your nuts (tee hee), and you can decide which you'd like to use, depending on the time you have. Always make sure to measure your cashews before softening, as they will increase in size once soaked. Use the soaked nuts right away, as they don't store well.

BOILING METHOD:

My favorite method as I am often short on time . . . (aka, lazy).
Put the cashews in a small saucepan and cover with plenty of water. Bring to a boil, and boil for 10 to 15 minutes until tender. Drain and rinse with cold water, and they are good to go!

SOAKING METHOD:

Place the cashews in a large bowl and cover generously with cool water. Let soak for a minimum of 2 hours, or as long as overnight. Drain and rinse with cold water before using.

Other nuts, such as macadamia, might take a little longer to soften, so do a taste test to ensure they are nice and tender all the way through.

Boil or soak

MORNING MUNCHIES

There are few things more challenging than finding vegan brunch options at a restaurant. Sure, it's easy to whip up a smoothie at home, make some oatmeal, or pour some soy milk over granola, but as soon as you hit the restaurant territory: Game over. Whomp whomp. Restaurants offer up plenty of bacon, sausages, and eggs prepared every which way, but even the less threatening-looking items such as pancakes, waffles, baked goods, and parfaits are filled with eggs and dairy. Sigh.

Never fear! I have excellent news for you: No need to go out for brunch at all! The recipes in this chapter cover all your morning munchie needs. Sweet, savory, easy to prepare, this will be the best brunch you have ever had. Now, pour yourself some coffee, pop some champagne for mimosas, and let's get to satisfying those morning munchies.

PILLOWY PANCAKES

No eggs, no dairy, and yet these will be the most pillowy-soft pancakes your mouth has ever encountered. These are so easy-peasy to make and they turn out superbly every time. Fluffy and light with that perfect slightly sweet pancake taste, buttermilk pancakes ain't got nothing on these, so you can toss the packaged mix. I promise, these will be your new favorite flapjack.

Prep time: 10 mins • Cook time: 20 mins • Makes: About 12 pancakes

DRY INGREDIENTS

1 ½ cups all-purpose flour

2 Tbsp white sugar

1 Tbsp baking powder

½ tsp salt

WET INGREDIENTS

1 ¾ cups non-dairy milk (such as soy or almond)

3 Tbsp light oil (such as canola or vegetable), plus more for frying

1 Tbsp fresh lemon juice

½ tsp vanilla extract

••••••• Amper-Uppers •••••••

When the pancakes are cooking on the first side, sprinkle some berries or cherries (my fave), some chocolate chips, or chopped nuts on top before flipping.

1. In a large bowl, whisk together all of the dry ingredients. Set aside.

2. In a medium bowl, whisk together all of the wet ingredients. Now pour the wet ingredients into the dry and mix until just combined. It's ok if there are lumps, just don't overmix the batter or you run the risk of killing the fluffiness.

3. Lightly oil a nonstick frying pan and put it over medium heat. When the pan is hot, use a ¼-cup measure to scoop the batter into the pan. Use the edge of the measuring cup or a spoon to spread the batter into nice pancake shapes.

4. Let cook for a couple of minutes. When large bubbles start showing up on the surface of the pancakes, and they're golden brown on the bottom, flip them and cook for an additional couple of minutes on the opposite side, until golden brown and cooked all the way through. You may have to adjust your heat as you go for the perfect pancake pan temperature.

5. Serve with your toppings of choice. I like sliced strawberries with maple syrup and vegan butter.

••••••••••••••••• Cool Tip •••••••••••••••••

Keep an oven-safe dish in an oven set at 150°F–200°F, and add pancakes to it as you make them. They'll stay warm until you're ready to eat.

DREAMY TOFU SCRAMBLE

Are you someone who once loved eggs and now misses having them at breakfast? Or perhaps you're like me and you hate eggs, but you love the idea of having tasty, dreamy tofu for breakfast? Either way, this scramble is a healthy breakfast option that will satisfy whatever your needs and keep you full all morning long.

Prep time: 10 mins • Cook time: 20 mins • Serves: 4

1 Tbsp vegan butter or olive oil

1 onion, chopped

4 cloves garlic, minced

1 block (14 oz) firm tofu

2 Tbsp nutritional yeast

½ tsp black salt or sea salt (or to taste)

¼ tsp ground turmeric

Handful of chives for garnish

1. Heat the vegan butter or oil in a nonstick frying pan over medium-high heat, and add the onion and garlic. Sauté until the onion becomes soft and just begins to brown.

2. Use your fingers to crumble up the tofu into the pan. Add the nutritional yeast, salt, and turmeric, and stir to combine. Cook until heated through, about 5 minutes. Garnish with chives and serve hot, with toast, if you like.

• • • • • • • • • Cool Tip • • • • • • • •

Wrap this tofu scramble up in a large tortilla with some rice, black beans, avocado, and salsa for a totally fab breakfast burrito. Serve with a dollop of Sour Cream of My Dreams (page 207) to take it to the next level.

• • • • • • • • • • • • • Amper-Uppers • • • • • • • • • • • • • •

One of the most awesome things about tofu scrambles is that they can be prepared in an endless number of ways with your favorite additions. Sauté some extra veggies along with the onions, add some cooked beans, toss in some fresh herbs, top with some vegan cheese or avocado. . . . Just use whatever you have on hand!

One warning, though. When it comes to amping up your scramble, more isn't always better. Pick and choose up to five of your favorite ingredients that go well together. Some combos I like are:

• Sweet peppers, black beans, and cilantro.
• Spinach, vegan mozzarella, and hot peppers.
• Sun-dried tomatoes, zucchini, and fresh basil.

OVERNIGHT CINNAMON BUN FRENCH TOAST BAKE

Having a bunch of guests stay the night? This is the perfect recipe to serve for breakfast the next morning. Prepare it the night before so all you have to do is pop it in the oven when you wake up, and you'll have plenty of time to just relax and drink your coffee while it bakes. It really tastes so decadent, just like biting into a warm cinnamon bun, icing and all.

Prep time: 15 mins (+ overnight to soak + 5 mins for the heavy cream)
Cook time: 25–30 mins • Serves: 8

FOR THE SAUCE

2 ripe bananas

1 cup full-fat coconut milk or Heavenly Heavy Cream (page 206)

1 cup non-dairy milk (such as soy or almond)

¼ cup brown sugar, packed

1 Tbsp cornstarch

1 Tbsp ground cinnamon

1 tsp vanilla extract

FOR THE FRENCH TOAST

1 lb loaf of day-old bread, cubed

1 cup pecans, roughly chopped

½ cup raisins

FOR THE ICING

1 cup icing sugar

2–3 Tbsp full-fat coconut milk or Heavenly Heavy Cream (page 206)

1. For the sauce, place all of the sauce ingredients in a blender and blend until smooth.

2. For the French toast, place the bread cubes in a 9- x 13-inch baking dish. Pour the sauce mixture over top and then stir so that all of the bread cubes soak up a bit of the sauce. Cover and put in the fridge overnight.

3. When you're ready to bake, preheat your oven to 350°F. Remove the French toast pan from the fridge and give it a stir. Sprinkle the raisins and pecans over top, then bake the French toast, uncovered, for 25–30 minutes, until the top is lightly browned.

4. Mix together the icing ingredients and drizzle about half of it over top. Use the remaining half to serve on the side.

• • • • • • • • • • • • • • • • Cool Tip • • • • • • • • • • • • • • • •

The key to this recipe is to make sure your bread is a little dried out. If the bread is too soft and fresh, you run the risk of soggy French toast.

EASY (BUT FANCY-LOOKING) TOFU FRITTATA

Is there anything more satisfying than pulling a big skillet of golden scrumptiousness like a tofu frittata out of the oven and serving it right from the pan? So rustic, so hip. Add a side of Insanely Good Rice Paper Bacon (page 26), a few slices of fresh avocado, and maybe some cheddar and chive scones, and oooh momma, breakfast is served! Not up for the challenge that early in the day? This also makes a lovely light summer dinner when served with a salad and a crisp glass of white wine.

Prep time: 20 mins • Cook time: 50 mins • Serves: 4-6

FOR THE FRITTATA MIXTURE

1 block (12 oz) extra-firm tofu

½ cup non-dairy milk (such as soy or almond)

3 Tbsp nutritional yeast

1 Tbsp cornstarch

¾ tsp ground turmeric

¾ tsp salt or black salt

FOR THE VEGGIES

1 Tbsp olive oil

½ yellow onion, chopped

½ red bell pepper, chopped

3 cloves garlic, minced

8 oz button mushrooms, sliced

4 cups fresh baby spinach

1. Preheat your oven to 375°F.

2. Break the tofu into pieces and place it in a food processor or blender along with the remaining frittata ingredients. Process until smooth and creamy. The mixture will be thick.

3. For the veggies, heat the olive oil in an oven-safe nonstick frying pan. When the oil is hot, add the onion, bell pepper, and garlic. Sauté until the onion softens and begins to brown. Add the mushrooms and continue to cook until they start to shrink and are cooked through. Add the spinach and stir until it's wilted. Remove the pan from the heat.

4. Pour the tofu into the pan and stir it into the sautéed veggies to mix. Using a spatula, make sure that the tofu is spread evenly in the pan.

5. Pop the pan in the oven and bake for 30–40 minutes, until the edges just begin to brown and the center is completely set. Let rest for 5–10 minutes before serving.

• Amper-Uppers • • • • • • • • • • • • • • • • • • •

Make this recipe into a quiche by simply spreading the prepared mixture into an unbaked pie crust (page 214) and baking at the same temperature and for the same time until the crust has lightly browned and the center of the quiche has set.

FALL-IN-LOVE BEET ⁙ CARROT LOX

There is a little vegan bakery near my house that serves beet lox on a toasted bagel. The first time I had it, I immediately fell in love with it and knew I had to make my own version. I've come up with two great options for you. The beet lox is rich in color and has a sweet, earthy taste, while the carrot lox is milder in flavor but has a real punch of seasoning (and bonus: it looks shockingly like traditional lox!).

Prep time: 10 mins • Cook time: 15 mins • Serves: 4

FOR THE LOX

2 medium carrots or beets, peeled

1 ½ Tbsp water

1 Tbsp soy sauce (gluten-free, if preferred)

2 tsp white miso paste

½ tsp liquid smoke

½ tsp garlic powder

FOR THE BAGELS

Ricotta I Like a Lot-a (page 205) or store-bought vegan cream cheese

4 bagels, cut in half and toasted (or gluten-free bread, if preferred)

½ yellow onion, thinly sliced

2 Tbsp capers

1. Preheat your oven to 400°F.

2. Use a potato peeler to slice the carrots or beets into long, thin strips. If you have a mandolin, you can use that.

3. In a small baking dish, mix together the water, soy sauce, miso paste, liquid smoke, and garlic powder. Add your carrot or beet strips, toss to combine, and then cover with foil. Bake for 10–15 minutes, tossing halfway through, until tender. You can serve this hot or cold. Keep leftover beet or carrot lox in an airtight container in the fridge.

4. Assemble the bagels by smearing some ricotta on the bagel halves and topping with slices of beet or carrot, followed by onion slices and capers.

•••••••• Amper-Uppers ••••••••

If you like the taste of the sea, grind up a sheet of nori (the seaweed that's used for making sushi) and stir it into the marinade to give the beets or carrots a briny taste.

•••••••••••••••••• Cool Tip ••••••••••••••••••

• The carrot and beet lox is also fab when used on top of pasta or in a salad.
• If you decide to make both beet and carrot lox at the same time, make sure to cook them in separate pans. The beets have such a strong color that they will stain the carrots if they touch.

INSANELY GOOD RICE PAPER BACON

Yes, bacon made from rice paper, the very same circular sheets you use to make cold spring rolls. Rice paper bacon hit the internet and took it by storm, and there is one very clear reason why: It's insanely good! It's by far the closest thing to traditional bacon I have ever encountered. Crispy, chewy, and smoky, all of the flavor friends are here to have a party in your mouth.

Prep time: 15 mins • Cook time: 10 mins • Makes: About 12 slices

3 Tbsp nutritional yeast

2 Tbsp light oil (such as canola or vegetable)

1 Tbsp soy sauce (gluten-free, if preferred)

½ tsp liquid smoke

½ tsp maple syrup

¼ tsp smoked paprika

¼ tsp garlic powder

6 sheets of extra-large rice paper

•••••••• Cool Tip ••••••••

I love using three layers of rice paper because I think that gives the perfect combo of crispy and chewy. For a crispier bacon, use two sheets, and for all chew (more on the jerky side of things), use four sheets.

1. Preheat your oven to 400°F. Line a baking sheet with parchment paper.

2. In a small casserole dish, mix everything except the rice paper together to make a marinade.

3. Take three sheets of the rice paper, very quickly run them under water, and then place them on top of each other. Let them sit for about 30 seconds to stick together. Use a large knife or kitchen scissors to cut them into strips about 2 inches wide. Now dunk each strip in the marinade. Use your finger to wipe the excess marinade off. To get the ultimate crispy and chewy texture, leave some parts with more marinade and some with less. Lay the strip on the prepared baking sheet. Repeat with the remaining strips. When you run out of strips, repeat the process with the other three sheets of rice paper.

4. Bake for 8–10 minutes, until the bacon bubbles and has browned up nicely.

5. You can double or triple the recipe as needed. Once cooked, the rice paper bacon will keep in an airtight container in the fridge for a few days. If it softens, you can crisp it back up by tossing it in a frying pan, over medium heat, for a few minutes.

Take 3 sheets of rice paper, run them under water, and lay them on top of each other.

>>

Let rest for 30 seconds until they stick together, then cut into strips.

>>

Take a strip and dunk it in the marinade. Use your fingers to wipe the excess off.

Bake on a parchment paper-lined baking sheet for 8 - 10 mintues for crispy, chewy deliciousness.

SENSATIONAL SMOKY TOFU & AVOCADO BENEDICT

I've never been a Benedict type of person, because even in my pre-vegan days, I never liked eggs, but I can tell you that I sure love THIS Benedict. It tastes just as sinfully rich as the traditional version, but the richness here comes from the creamy avocado and a thick tofu slice that is slightly sweet and a little bit smoky. I'm drooling as I'm writing this . . . for real.

Prep time: 1 hour to overnight to marinate • Cook time: 10 mins • Serves: 4

FOR THE TOFU

1 block (12 oz) extra-firm tofu, pressed (see page 10), and cut into 8 slices

2 Tbsp olive oil, plus more for frying

2 Tbsp maple syrup

2 Tbsp soy sauce (gluten-free, if preferred)

1 tsp liquid smoke

½ tsp garlic powder

½ tsp chili powder

FOR THE HOLLANDAISE

¼ cup vegan butter or coconut oil

¼ cup flour (all-purpose or gluten-free all-purpose flour blend)

2 cups non-dairy milk (such as soy or almond)

2 Tbsp nutritional yeast

2 Tbsp fresh lemon juice

2 tsp agave or maple syrup

½ tsp black salt or sea salt

¼ tsp ground turmeric

TO ASSEMBLE

4 English muffins, sliced in half and toasted (gluten-free, if preferred)
2 avocados, sliced

1. Place the olive oil, maple syrup, soy sauce, liquid smoke, garlic powder, and chili powder in a large resealable plastic bag. Add the pressed tofu slices and make sure they are well covered. Marinate in the fridge for a minimum of 15 minutes, but overnight works best for optimal flavor.

2. Add a bit of oil to a frying pan, and put over medium-high heat, and when hot, add the tofu. Cook for about 3 minutes per side, until golden brown.

3. For the hollandaise, melt the vegan butter in a saucepan over medium heat. Whisk in the flour to form a paste and cook for 1 minute, whisking constantly. Add the non-dairy milk, nutritional yeast, lemon juice, agave, salt, and turmeric, and whisk well to combine. Cook about 5 minutes until thickened. If you find it gets too thick, just splash in a little more milk and whisk to combine.

4. To assemble, put a slice of the fried tofu on half a toasted English muffin, then top with a couple of avocado slices. Generously drizzle with warm hollandaise sauce and await the delighted groans from the breakfast table. You're welcome.

Other delicious Benedict topping additions:
• Basil or chives • Grilled zucchini •
• Sautéed spinach •
Insanely Good Rice Paper Bacon (page 26) •
• Thick slices of tomato

BLUEBERRY BLISS MUFFINS

As soon as the weather starts moving from summer to crisp fall, I start baking. It's almost an instinct, like hybernation, except for me it's more like *carbernation*. These blueberry muffins always hit the spot. While fresh blueberries are fab for these, they can be made with frozen ones, so you can have the perfect baked good for any time of year.

Prep time: 10 mins • Cook time: 15-22 mins • Makes: 8-9 large bakery-style muffins or 12 small muffins

DRY INGREDIENTS

1 ½ cups all-purpose flour

¾ cup white sugar

2 tsp baking powder

½ tsp salt

WET INGREDIENTS

¾ cup non-dairy milk (such as soy or almond)

½ cup light oil (such as canola or vegetable oil)

1 Tbsp fresh lemon juice

2 tsp vanilla extract

1 cup blueberries (fresh or frozen)

1. Preheat your oven to 400°F. Lightly grease the cups of a muffin pan or fill it with liners.

2. In a large bowl, whisk together all of the dry ingredients. Set aside.

3. In a medium bowl, whisk together all of the wet ingredients except for the blueberries. Pour the wet ingredients into the dry ingredients and mix until just combined. Add the blueberries and lightly fold them in, being careful not to overmix. It's ok if there are lumps.

4. For large bakery-style muffins, fill 8–9 muffin cups right to the top with batter, then bake for 18–22 minutes until lightly golden on top, and a toothpick inserted in the center of a muffin comes out clean. For small muffins, divide the batter evenly among the 12 muffin cups and bake for 15–20 minutes, until lightly golden on top and a toothpick inserted in the center of a muffin comes out clean. Let the muffins cool in the pan, then store them on a plate covered with a clean tea towel for 2 to 3 days. This will keep the muffins the best texture, but if you want them to last longer, store them in a large sealable bag in the fridge for up to a week.

HEAVENLY FRENCH TOAST

Slightly crispy on the outside and creamy on the inside, this French toast is heavenly and takes just a couple of minutes to whip up. You can use any kind of bread you like, but I always look for a fluffy French bread that I can cut into thick slices.

Prep time: 10 mins • Cook time: 20 mins • Makes: 4–6 slices

½ cup non-dairy milk (such as soy or almond)

½ cup full-fat coconut milk (shaken well before measuring)

1 ½ Tbsp cornstarch

1 Tbsp maple syrup or agave

1 tsp vanilla extract

½ tsp ground cinnamon

4–6 thick slices of day-old bread

1. In a small casserole dish wide enough to fit a slice of bread, whisk together the non-dairy and coconut milk, cornstarch, maple syrup, vanilla, and cinnamon. Make sure the cornstarch is whisked in well and fully dissolved.

2. Lightly oil a nonstick frying pan with a light oil like canola or vegetable, and put it over medium heat. While it's warming, dip a slice of bread into the liquid mixture, then flip and dip the other side so that the mixture is soaked through the bread. Shake off any excess, then put the soaked bread into your hot pan.

3. Fry for 2–3 minutes on each side, until golden brown on both sides and soft in the middle. Serve hot with your favorite toppings, and you've got yourself one mighty fine breakfast feast.

• • • • • • • Vegan Tidbit • • • • • • •

Most bread is vegan, but always double-check the label to make sure there are no eggs or milk hiding in there.

• • • • • • • • • • • • • • • • • • Cool Tip • • • • • • • • • • • • • • •

The key to perfect French toast is to make sure your bread is slightly dried out. If the bread is too soft and fresh, you run the risk of a soggy dish.

PUMPKIN SPICE PANCAKE PERFECTION

I'm pretty sure I was in love with pumpkin spice before it was hip. Yeah, I'm that kind of cool, you know it. If you love pumpkin spice lattes, you'll love these pancakes. I made this recipe for a special someone one morning, and not only was he wowed that they were indeed vegan, he had four helpings . . . Yes, four!

Prep time: 10 mins • Cook time: 20 mins • Makes: About 12 pancakes

DRY INGREDIENTS

1 ½ cups all-purpose flour

¼ cup white sugar

1 Tbsp baking powder

2 tsp pumpkin pie spice

WET INGREDIENTS

1 ¼ cups non-dairy milk (such as soy or almond)

¾ cup pumpkin purée (not pumpkin pie filling)

3 Tbsp light oil (such as canola or vegetable), plus more for frying

1 Tbsp fresh lemon juice

½ tsp vanilla extract

•••••••• Cool Tip ••••••••

These pancakes have a gorgeous golden color that makes them perfect for Halloween. If you're feeling really festive, make very cute jack-o'-lantern faces with chocolate chips on the raw side of the pancake before flipping. Too cute for words . . . Wait. No, they're not. I have a word: YUM!

1. In a large bowl, whisk together all of the dry ingredients.

2. In a medium bowl, whisk together all of the wet ingredients. Now pour the wet ingredients into the dry and stir until just combined. Lumps are totally cool; just don't overmix, or you may ruin the fluffiness of the pancakes.

3. Lightly oil a nonstick frying pan and put it over medium heat. When the pan is hot, use a ¼-cup measure to scoop the batter into pancake shapes in the pan. The batter will be thicker than traditional pancake batter, but trust me on this. Use the edge of the measuring cup or a spoon to spread the batter into nice pancake shapes.

4. Let cook for a couple of minutes. When large bubbles start showing up on the surface, and they're golden brown on the bottom, flip them and cook for an additional couple of minutes on the opposite side, until golden brown and cooked all the way through. You may have to adjust your heat as you go for the perfect pancake pan temperature.

5. Serve with your toppings of choice. I like Magical Coconut Whipped Cream (page 181) and a drizzle of maple syrup.

EXTRA-BANANA-Y BANANA BREAD

Can you ever go wrong with banana bread? The answer is no. Banana bread is always a good idea, and this banana bread is seriously the best ever! Not only is it super moist and banana-y, like a good banana bread should be, but I fold extra chunks of banana and chopped walnuts into the batter, making this like no banana bread you have ever encountered.

Prep time: 10 mins • Cook time: 55-65 mins • Makes: 1 (8- x 4-inch) loaf (serves 12)

DRY INGREDIENTS

1 cup whole wheat flour

1 cup all-purpose flour

2 tsp baking powder

1 tsp ground cinnamon

¼ tsp salt

WET INGREDIENTS

1 ⅓ cups mashed banana (about 3 bananas)

½ light oil (such as canola or vegetable)

½ cup white sugar

¼ cup brown sugar

1 Tbsp lemon zest

1 Tbsp fresh lemon juice

1 tsp vanilla extract

ADD-INS

1 medium ripe banana, cut into chunks

1 cup roughly chopped walnuts (optional, but highly recommended)

1. Preheat your oven to 350°F. Lightly grease an 8- x 4-inch loaf pan.

2. In a large bowl, mix together all of the dry ingredients. Set aside.

3. In another large bowl, mix together all of the wet ingredients. Add the wet ingredients to the dry ingredients and mix until just combined. Fold in the chopped banana and the walnuts (if using). Dump the batter into the prepared loaf pan and smooth the top of it.

4. Pop it in the oven and bake for 55–65 minutes, until a toothpick inserted into the center comes out clean. Let cool for 10–15 minutes before removing from the pan. For optimal freshness, let the banana bread cool and store at room temperature covered with a clean tea towel for 2 to 3 days. For longer storage, cover the loaf pan with foil or plastic wrap and keep in the fridge for up to a week.

························· Cool Tip ·························
If you're using a cookie cutter to make round scones, press it straight down, then pull it straight up. Twisting the cookie cutter will stop the scones from rising as much.

BETTER-THAN-BAKERY CHEDDAR & CHIVE SCONES

There is a little coffee shop around the corner from my house that makes the most scrumptious cheddar and chive scones . . . That is, they *were* the most scrumptious until I went vegan. At first I was really bummed I could no longer indulge in this special treat, but as you know, I quickly learned that anything can be made vegan and taste even better than the original. These scones prove it! They're buttery, cheesy, and all things that don't seem very vegan.

30 minutes or less   **SUPER SIMPLE**

Prep time: 10 mins • Cook time: 14-17 mins • Makes: 8-12 scones

DRY INGREDIENTS

2 cups all-purpose flour

2 tsp white sugar

2 tsp baking powder

1 tsp garlic powder

½ tsp baking soda

½ tsp salt

¼ tsp black pepper

WET INGREDIENTS

½ cup vegan butter

½ cup non-dairy milk (such as soy or almond)

1 Tbsp fresh lemon juice

¼ cup chopped chives

½ cup Nacho Cheese Love (page 201), chilled for at least ½ an hour to overnight prior to using

1. Preheat your oven to 400°F. Line a baking sheet with parchment paper.

2. In a large bowl, mix together all of the dry ingredients. Cut the vegan butter into small cubes or pieces and drop them into the dry mixture. Use a fork or pastry cutter to cut the vegan butter into the flour until the flour reaches a sandy texture.

3. In a medium bowl, mix together the non-dairy milk and lemon juice. It will curdle, so don't panic. Add this to the dry ingredients and stir until just combined. Before the dough is completely mixed, add the chives, and use a tablespoon to scoop small blobs of the cold nacho cheese into the dough. Gently mix until the dough just comes together. Do not overmix. There should be dollops of nacho cheese visible throughout the mixture.

4. Lightly flour a clean work surface, and put the dough on top. Use your hands to pat the dough into a flat circle, about 1 inch thick. Either use a large round cookie cutter to make circular scones, or cut the dough like a pizza into eight triangular scones. Space them out on the prepared baking sheet. Bake for 14–17 minutes, until they have risen slightly and are browned on the bottom. Scones are best the day they are made, but you can revive these a day or two later by slicing in half, toasting, and adding a smear of vegan butter. Store any leftovers in an airtight container at room temperature for a few days.

GOOD MORNING APPLE CINNAMON MUFFINS

This muffin is so much fun! (Yes, muffins can totally be fun.) Not only is it bursting with cinnamon and surprising little bites of sweet apple throughout, but the top of each is dipped into cinnamon sugar. It reminds me of how, when I was a kid, I used to make cinnamon toast for breakfast.

Prep time: 20 mins • Cook time: 15-22 mins • Makes: 8-9 large bakery-style muffins or 12 small muffins

DRY INGREDIENTS

1 ½ cups all-purpose flour

¾ cup white sugar

2 tsp baking powder

2 tsp ground cinnamon

½ tsp salt

WET INGREDIENTS

¾ cup non-dairy milk (such as soy or almond)

½ cup light oil (such as canola or vegetable oil)

1 Tbsp fresh lemon juice

1 tsp vanilla extract

1 ½ cups apples (diced into roughly ¼-inch cubes), Cortlands and Granny Smith are my go-to's, but any apple will do

CINNAMON SUGAR TOPPING

2 Tbsp white sugar

1 tsp ground cinnamon

2 Tbsp melted vegan butter

1. Preheat your oven to 400°F. Lightly grease a muffin pan or fill it with liners.

2. In a large bowl, whisk together all of the dry ingredients. Set aside.

3. In a medium bowl, whisk together all of the wet ingredients, except for the apples. Pour the wet ingredients into the dry ingredients and mix until just combined. Don't overmix the batter or your muffins might not rise properly. Lumps are totally fine.

4. Gently fold in the apples. For large and in-charge muffins, fill 8–9 muffin cups to the top with batter and bake for 18–22 minutes, until a toothpick inserted into the center of a muffin comes out clean, and the tops are lightly golden. For smaller muffins, divide the batter evenly among the 12 muffin cups and then bake for 15–20 minutes, until lightly golden in color and a toothpick inserted into the center of a muffin comes out clean. Remove from the oven and let the muffins cool completely before topping.

5. To make the topping, mix together the sugar and cinnamon in a small bowl just big enough to fit a muffin. Use a pastry brush to brush some of the melted butter on the top of the muffin, then dip the muffin into the cinnamon sugar to coat the top. Repeat with the remaining muffins. Let the muffins cool in the pan. To keep them at the best texture, store them on a plate covered with a clean tea towel on the counter for 2 to 3 days. If you want to keep them longer, put them in a sealable bag in the fridge for up to a week.

EASY-PEASY CRÊPES

As a kid, I was always more of a crêpe person than a pancake person. Yep, this kid had style! Put a beret on me and . . . Wait, I really did wear a beret. Nope, I'm not French. I'm just classy like that.

Back to crêpes. When I was a very cool teen, I used to make them for my friends on the weekends. I felt like a superstar when my friends oohed and ahhed over how fancy they seemed. Well, I've got news for you: Crêpes are so easy! I actually find them easier to make than pancakes, because you don't need exceptional flipping skills. Can I get a fist pump for that? (Are fist pumps classy?)

Prep time: 10 mins • Cook time: 20 mins • Makes: About 6 crêpes

1 ½ cups non-dairy milk (such as soy or almond)

1 cup all-purpose flour

3 Tbsp light oil (such as vegetable or canola), plus more for the pan

1 Tbsp white sugar

¼ tsp salt

1. Place everything in a blender or a large bowl and blend or whisk well to combine. Let the batter rest for 5–10 minutes.

2. Lightly oil a nonstick frying pan and put it over medium heat. When the pan is hot, pour about ⅓ cup batter into it and quickly swirl the batter around in a thin layer. Let cook for a couple of minutes until the very edges start to become crispy and golden brown. This is your cue that the crêpe is ready to flip. Flip it, and cook for another couple of minutes until golden on both sides. Serve hot with toppings of choice.

• • • • • • • • • • • • • •   Amper-Uppers   • • • • • • • • • • • • • •

I love my crêpes with a squeeze of lemon and a sprinkle of sugar, but feel free to jazz them up any way you like. You could have them with maple syrup and vegan butter, or peanut butter and banana, or berries and Magical Coconut Whipped Cream (page 181). Or you can go savory and add sautéed mushrooms and vegan mozzarella cheese (page 200), or sautéed spinach and Ricotta I Like a Lot-a (page 205) . . . The possibilities are endlessly scrumptious!

SUPER-SIMPLE CHOCOLATE CHIP GRANOLA BARS

Granola bars are great to grab when I'm zipping out the door—they make breakfast easy! But, for some annoying reason, a good majority of store-bought granola bars contain milk ingredients, which, of course, makes them not vegan. This recipe solves that problem. Even better, these bars are super easy to whip up—no baking involved!

Prep time: 10 mins + 2 hours to chill • Cook time: 5 mins
Makes: About 12 granola bars

¼ cup agave

¼ cup brown sugar

¼ cup vegan butter or coconut oil

1 tsp vanilla extract

¼ tsp salt

2 ½ cups rolled oats (gluten-free, if preferred)

¼ cup mini vegan chocolate chips

1. Line an 8- x 8-inch square baking pan with parchment paper or plastic wrap, with some hanging over the sides to make handles.

2. Place the agave, brown sugar, vegan butter, vanilla, and salt in a saucepan over medium heat and bring to a simmer. Simmer for about 2 minutes, whisking constantly.

3. Remove from the heat and stir in the oats. Let cool for about 5 minutes, then gently mix in half of the chocolate chips. They might melt a bit, but that's ok. Scoop the mixture into the prepared baking pan and flatten with a spatula, compacting the oats firmly. Sprinkle the remaining chocolate chips over top and lightly pat them down. Let cool, uncovered, in the fridge for about 2 hours until chilled. Remove from the pan and cut into bars. Store in an airtight container in the fridge for up to a week.

• • • • • • • • • • • • • • • Cool Tip • • • • • • • • • • • • • • •

If chocolate chips aren't your thang, replace them with any chopped nut or dried fruit of your choice. Note, though, that the bars may be a bit more crumbly.

BEST-EVER WAFFLES

These waffles are hands down the best waffles I have ever had, vegan or not. Lightly crispy on the outside, gloriously fluffy on the inside, and slightly sweet all the way through, these are pure waffle-y perfection.

Prep time: 10 mins • Cook time: 20 mins • Makes: 4-6 waffles

2 cups all-purpose flour

¼ cup white sugar

1 Tbsp baking powder

¼ tsp salt

1 ¾ cups non-dairy milk (such as soy or almond)

½ cup light oil (such as canola or vegetable)

1 Tbsp fresh lemon juice

1 tsp vanilla extract

Oil for waffle iron

1. Heat your waffle iron so it's ready to go when your batter is ready.

2. In a large bowl, whisk together the flour, sugar, baking powder, and salt. Now add the non-dairy milk, oil, lemon juice, and vanilla, then mix together until just combined. Lumps are totally cool.

3. When the waffle iron is hot, spray oil or lightly brush oil on both the top and bottom griddles of the waffle iron, then scoop your batter and spread it around so that it just covers the griddle, leaving room for the batter to expand.

4. Close the waffle iron, and cook until the waffle is golden on both sides. Use a fork to help release the waffle. Continue cooking the remaining waffles. My favorite way to serve hot waffle is with a dollop of coconut whipped cream (page 181), fresh berries, and a drizzle of maple syrup.

• • • • • • • • • • • • • • • • • • Cool Tip • • • • • • • • • • • • • • • • • •

If you want to make a big batch of waffles and freeze them for on-the-go, easy breakfasts, just line a baking sheet with parchment paper, lay out your waffles in a single layer on the sheet, and put in your freezer. Once they are frozen, you can move them to a freezer bag or container. To heat up, pop in your toaster!

Blueberry waffles, chocolate chip waffles, banana-walnut waffles, cheesy waffles . . .
The combinations are endless. But what happens when one person loves strawberries, and
another person only wants a drizzle of peanut butter? You fight. To the death.

Kidding!

With this fun little trick you can give each waffle a unique flavor. In fact, each waffle can have four
separate flavors if that's what you're up for! Working quickly, just pour a thin layer of waffle batter
into the waffle iron, sprinkle a small amount of whatever your favorite topping is over top of the
batter (each section can be different), then cover it all up with another thin layer of waffle
batter. Close the iron, let it cook, and hidden treasures can be found in every bite!

Banana slices • Berries (any kind) • Chocolate chips • Chopped nuts • Coconut flakes
Vegan cheese • Peanut butter (or other nut butters) • Any other awesome ideas you come up with!

Mix up that batta!

Spread a thin layer of
batter over the waffle iron.
Add toppings of choice.
Top with another thin layer
of batter,
and
cook it up.

OMNOMNOMNOMNOM!!!

Get the
PARTY
STARTED

When I began writing a cookbook, I knew 100% that one recipe I was not going to include was hummus. Nobody needs to tell a vegan they can eat hummus. I mean, come on, we can do better than that. Don't get me wrong, I love hummus AND guacamole, but they can get a bit boring and predictable. So, I've come up with a chapter full of exquisite appetizers that will woo the most non-vegan person, but also happen to go exceptionally well with wine, friends, and rom-coms.

POPPIN' JALAPEÑO POPPERS

Before I first tasted a jalapeño popper, I was a little nervous. Eating half a jalapeño in just one bite? My mouth would be on fire, surely. Not true! Jalapeños can be quite spicy when raw, but cooking them kills most of the spiciness, making them almost sweet, with just a kick of spice at the end. My version of these has the jalapeños stuffed with my favorite vegan mozzarella, then topped with coconut bacon or crushed tortilla chips for a bit of crunch. Yaaasss!

Prep time: 15 mins • Cook time: 18-20 mins (+ 7 mins for the mozzarella)
Makes: 12 jalapeño poppers

6 jalapeños, sliced in half lengthwise (seeds and membrane scraped out and discarded)

1 recipe Life-Changing Mozzarella (page 200)

2 Tbsp Addictive Coconut Bacon Bits (page 210) or crushed tortilla chips

1. Preheat your oven to 375°F. Line a baking pan with a wire rack.

2. Fill the jalapeños with the mozzarella, then nestle them between the wires of the wire rack in the baking pan, with the filling facing up. The space in between each wire is perfect for holding the jalapeños upright, stopping them from tipping over.

3. Bake for 18–20 minutes, until the jalapeños are cooked through. To get a nice brown top, crank your oven to broil for 30 seconds to 1 minute. Watch the jalapeños carefully—they can burn quickly! Remove from the oven, sprinkle immediately with the coconut bacon or tortilla chips, and serve hot.

• • • • • • • • • • • • • • • Vegan Tidbit • • • • • • • • • • • • • • •

When working with hot peppers, always wear rubber gloves. You'll notice if you don't wear gloves when you stick your finger in your eye later on. (I learned this from experience!)

SUPREME SPINACH ARTICHOKE DIP

In case you were wondering, the answer is yes. Yes, you should make and devour this immediately. This dip has become one of the most popular recipes on my blog, and the reason is simple: Pure deliciousness. I've amped it up a little here by sautéing the onion, garlic, and spinach, which makes it even better than it was. This is the kind of scrumptious comfort food dip you need to get through ANY and EVERY party, social occasion, and friends stopping by. Be prepared to say, "Yes, this really is vegan" over and over again.

Prep time: 5 mins • **Cook time:** 23 mins (+ 7 mins for the mozzarella) • **Serves:** 6

1 Tbsp olive oil

¼ yellow onion, finely chopped

2 cloves garlic, minced

4 cups fresh baby spinach

1 recipe Life-Changing Mozzarella (page 200)

1 jar (6 oz) marinated artichoke hearts, drained and roughly chopped

½ cup non-dairy milk (such as soy or almond), plus up to ½ cup more if needed

¼ tsp salt

¼ tsp black pepper

1. Preheat your oven to 400°F.

2. In an oven-safe frying pan, heat the olive oil over medium heat. Sauté the onion and garlic until softened and beginning to brown. Add the spinach and continue to sauté until the spinach is cooked down and reduced in size, 3–5 minutes. Turn off the heat. Add the mozzarella, artichoke hearts, ½ cup non-dairy milk, salt, and pepper and stir. It won't really come together yet, but don't worry.

3. Pop it in the oven for 20 minutes, giving it a stir halfway through cooking. If it's too thick, thin it by mixing in the extra non-dairy milk, 1 Tbsp at a time until desired consistency is reached.

4. Once the dip is fully cooked, you can brown the top by broiling for 1–3 minutes. Keep an eye on it so that it doesn't burn—it browns fast! Serve hot with bread, chips, or veggies.

THE CUTEST MINI MUSHROOM SLIDERS

Why are mini burgers so cute? I just want to eat 'em all up. You can make my Boss BBQ Veggie Burgers (page 93) or Scrumptious Sun-Dried Tomato & Walnut Bean Balls (page 126) into sliders if you like, but when it comes to appetizers, I prefer to keep things a little easier. I love these mini mushroom sliders because they're so simple to make. All you need are some mushrooms, and this awesome marinade.

Prep time: 15 mins (+ 30 mins–2 days to marinate) • Cook time: 10–25 mins
Makes: 8 sliders

FOR THE MARINADE

¼ cup olive oil

2 Tbsp soy sauce (gluten-free, if preferred)

1 Tbsp balsamic vinegar

½ tsp liquid smoke

1 tsp garlic powder

¼ tsp black pepper

FOR THE SLIDERS

8 mushrooms with caps that are just a little bigger than your buns (small portobellos or large criminis work well)

8 mini burgers buns or dinner rolls (or gluten-free buns, if preferred)

1. For the marinade, mix all the ingredients together in a medium bowl or sealable plastic bag.

2. For the sliders, slice off the stems of the clean mushrooms so you have just the caps. Add the mushrooms to the marinade, and toss to coat well. Let marinate for at least 30 minutes (or as long as 2 days if kept in the fridge).

3. You can choose to either bake or grill the mushrooms. To bake, preheat your oven to 375°F. Place the mushrooms on a baking sheet and pour any remaining marinade over them. Bake for 20–25 minutes, stopping to flip them halfway through, until the mushrooms are cooked through. To grill, cook the mushrooms for 2–5 minutes per side on a heated grill, until nice char marks form and the mushrooms are cooked through.

4. To assemble the sliders, place a mushroom and any toppings you like on the bottom half of each bun, and then follow with the top of the bun. If they have a hard time staying stacked up, you can use a decorative toothpick to hold them together.

PIZZA DOUGH PRETZEL BITES

If you have leftover pizza dough from last night's dinner, or if you are just ready to make a super-yum party-pleasing treat, these pretzel bites are just the thing. I sometimes make these just for myself as a movie-watching snack. Dip them in a little maple mustard sauce and you're singing (well, probably munching).

Prep time: 10 mins (+ 1 hour 15 mins for the pizza dough) • Cook time: 20-28 mins
Serves: 4

FOR THE PRETZEL BITES

⅓ cup baking soda

½ recipe Go-To Pizza Dough (page 211) or store-bought

¼ cup non-dairy milk (such as soy or almond)

Coarse salt (optional)

FOR THE MAPLE MUSTARD SAUCE

¼ cup Mayonnaise for Days (page 208) or store-bought vegan mayo

¼ cup Dijon mustard

2 Tbsp maple syrup

¼ tsp salt

1. Preheat your oven to 425°F. Line a baking sheet with parchment paper.

2. For the pretzel bites, bring a very large saucepan of water to a boil. You want lots of room for the pretzel bites to move around so they don't stick together. Once the water is boiling, stir in the baking soda. Be careful, as it will bubble and foam—oooh, science-y!

3. In the meantime, take small pieces of dough and roll them into little knots. The balls will double in size once cooked, so keep them fairly small, about the size of a cherry. Put the pretzel bites into the boiling water and boil for 2–5 minutes, until they begin to float. Remove from the saucepan with a slotted spoon and shake off excess water. Spread them out on the prepared baking sheet. Brush them with the non-dairy milk. Now sprinkle a tiny pinch of salt (if using) over them. Bake for 18–23 minutes, until golden brown.

4. For the sauce, place all the sauce ingredients in a small bowl and mix. Serve with the pretzel bites as a dip.

• • • • • • • • • • • • • • • • Vegan Tidbit • • • • • • • • • • • • • • • •

The baking soda in the water is what gives the pretzel bites their golden brown color. Without it, they would just be like balls of pizza crust.

OH MOMMY UMAMI LETTUCE WRAPS

I recently became addicted to lettuce wraps. This is serious, guys. I started shoving almost everything I could into lettuce leaves. I was going through an entire head of lettuce a day. Ok, ok, I know that's so super-vegan-sounding, but sometimes eating like a rabbit is actually a really tasty experience. This is my favorite lettuce filler combo: Asian-inspired seasoning with added texture from the walnuts, all wrapped in crunchy fresh lettuce. This rabbit cooks a mighty fine meal.

Prep time: 10 mins • Cook time: 10 mins • Serves: 4

FOR THE SAUCE

¼ cup soy sauce (gluten-free, if preferred)

2 Tbsp rice vinegar

2 Tbsp agave or maple syrup

2 tsp sesame oil

½ tsp your favorite hot sauce (optional)

FOR THE LENTILS

1 Tbsp light oil, like peanut or canola oil

1 yellow onion, chopped

3 cloves garlic, minced

1-inch piece fresh ginger, peeled and minced

1 cup red lentils

2 cups vegetable broth

½ cup walnuts, chopped

TO SERVE

1 head of butter lettuce or iceberg lettuce, leaves separated but kept whole

1 medium carrot, cut into matchsticks or grated

2 green onions, chopped

2 Tbsp toasted sesame seeds

1. For the sauce, in a small bowl, mix the ingredients together and set aside.

2. For the lentils, heat the oil in a frying pan over medium-high heat. When hot, add the onion, garlic, and ginger and sauté for about 5 minutes, until the onion softens and begins to brown.

3. Stir in the lentils and then the vegetable broth. Turn the heat to medium-low, cover, and simmer for about 10 minutes, until all the broth is absorbed and the lentils are cooked. Stir in the walnuts and about half of the sauce mixture, or to taste.

4. To serve, take a leaf of lettuce, fill it with the lentil-walnut mixture, top with carrot, green onions, and sesame seeds, and spoon as much sauce as desired over it all. Fold it like a taco and munch away!

CROWD-PLEASING JALAPEÑO CHEESE BALL

This gorgeous creation is a perfect make-ahead appetizer that will absolutely wow your friends. The combination of the cashews and coconut oil make it so smooth and creamy, it's kind of ridiculous. Even people who don't like cheese balls generally like THIS cheese ball.

 Prep time: 1 hour 15 mins (+ minimum chilling time) • Makes: 1 cheese ball (serves about 8)

1 cup raw cashews, softened (see page 13)

2 Tbsp nutritional yeast

2 Tbsp fresh lemon juice

2 Tbsp coconut oil

2 tsp white miso paste

1 clove garlic

1 tsp smoked paprika

¼ tsp ground turmeric

¼ tsp salt

½–1 jalapeño (depending on your spice preference), minced

½ cup sliced almonds

1. Add the softened cashews to a food processor along with the nutritional yeast, lemon juice, coconut oil, miso paste, garlic, paprika, turmeric, and salt. Blend until very smooth and creamy, stopping to scrape down the sides as needed. Now add the jalapeño, and pulse a few times to combine.

2. Line a small bowl with plastic wrap, and scoop the cheese mixture into the bowl. Gather up the sides of the plastic wrap and twist to form a ball and seal the top. Let the cheese ball firm up in the freezer for about an hour, or for a couple of hours in the fridge, or overnight.

3. Remove the now firm cheese ball from the plastic wrap and press the almonds onto the outside of the ball. You can also lightly press the ball to get a rounder shape if desired. You can serve it right away, or keep the cheese ball covered in the fridge for up to a week until you are ready to serve.

• • • • • • • • • • • • • •   Cool Tip   • • • • • • • • • • • • • •

Hate jalapeño? No problem. Just skip it, but you'd better rename the recipe or you might confuse people!

PERFECT PIZZA POCKETS

Do we even need to discuss these? Pizza pockets. What more needs to be said? All my favorite toppings shoved into fluffy dough and baked into a gooey, saucy, hand-held edible. I kind of feel like a kid in all the best possible ways when I eat these.

Basil and sun-dried tomatoes are my favorite pizza pocket fillings, but feel free to use whatever you want—mushrooms, onions, olives, pineapple, spinach, and artichokes are all delicious. Just make sure to not overfill these guys or they'll explode in the oven!

Prep time: 10 mins (+ 1 hour 15 mins for the pizza dough) • Cook time: 20 mins
Makes: 6 pizza pockets

1 recipe Go-To Pizza Dough (page 211) or store-bought pizza dough

¾ cup My Family Favorite Tomato Sauce (page 156) or store-bought

1 recipe Life-Changing Mozzarella (page 200)

Small handful of fresh basil leaves, roughly chopped

¼ cup sliced sun-dried tomatoes

¼ cup non-dairy milk (such as soy or almond) or olive oil

1. Preheat your oven to 425°F. Lightly grease a large baking sheet.

2. Cut the pizza dough into six evenly sized pieces. Take one of the pieces and stretch it into an oval about 5 x 8 inches. It doesn't have to be perfect at all, a rough shape is just fine. Repeat with the remaining pieces of dough.

3. Now it's time to fill your pizza pockets! Working with one piece of dough at a time, spread about 2 Tbsp tomato sauce on one half of the dough, and then top with some blobs of the cheese, a sprinkle of basil, and some sun-dried tomatoes. Make sure to keep the filling about an inch away from the edges of the dough so the edges can stick together properly. Fold the other half of the dough over the filling to make a pocket. Now seal up the edges by pinching them together and folding them up a bit on themselves. To make sure it's well sealed, go over the edges again with a fork to crimp them closed. Now use your fork to poke just a couple of holes in the top of the pizza pocket so the steam can escape during cooking. Repeat with the remaining dough and filling.

4. Lightly brush the tops of the pockets with the non-dairy milk or olive oil. Bake for 15–20 minutes, until nice and golden on the bottom and top. Careful, they will be hot!

•••••••••• Cool Tip ••••••••••

You can freeze the baked pizza pockets by wrapping them individually in plastic wrap and then storing them together in an airtight bag or container for up to a month. To reheat from frozen, preheat your oven to 400°F and bake for 16–18 minutes.

THE ULTIMATE 8-LAYER DIP

There is a big problem with this dip: It's really difficult to stop eating it! I seriously ate nothing but this dip for dinner the first time I made it. Good thing it's actually pretty healthy, and in my not so humble opinion, it's several notches above the classic non-vegan layer dip in the flavor department. You can serve this in a clear glass dish, or in stacked layers on a plate. You may have some leftovers if you go that way (not that that's a bad thing).

Prep time: 15 mins • Serves: About 12

1 can (14 oz) refried beans (check to make sure it's vegan)

2 avocados

1 Tbsp fresh lime juice

½ tsp salt

1 cup raw cashews, softened (see page 13)

1 orange bell pepper, deseeded and roughly chopped

⅓ cup water

¼ cup nutritional yeast

2 cups salsa (16 oz jar)

½ cucumber, chopped

2 cups cooked corn kernels, thawed if they were frozen

½ cup sliced black olives

2 green onions, chopped

1. Spread the refried beans evenly across the bottom of a 9- x 13-inch dish, a taller glass trifle dish, or a large plate.

2. Scoop out the flesh of the avocados into a bowl. Add the lime juice and salt and use a fork to mash it all together until smooth. Spread overtop of the refried beans.

3. Place the cashews, bell pepper, water, and nutritional yeast in a blender. Blend until smooth and creamy. Pour the mixture over the avocado and use a spatula to spread it out evenly.

4. Spread the salsa across the cashew mixture, followed by the cucumber, corn kernels, olives, and green onion.

SOUPS & SALADS

One thing that has really changed for me over the last few years is that I moved my salads from little side dishes to humongous troughs of greenery. I actually use a mixing bowl as my own personal salad bowl. Am I crazy? Maybe. Do I love it? Absolutely. You know the saying, "A trough a day keeps the doctor away"? Well, ok, no one says that, BUT I assure you, every doctor out there would support you eating an abundance of leafy greens everyday.

In the winter, my go-to trough doesn't appeal to me as much, but I still love packing in as many veggies as possible, so soups become my new favorite. Warm, comforting goodness paired with a vegan grilled cheese, or simply a crusty baguette. I always make big potfuls and freeze some for later, a perfect backup for those lazy nights or impromptu dinner parties.

DUDE-APPROVED BBQ CHICKPEA SALAD

Leafy greens make your body feel great, but most of the men I know aren't crazy about having salad for dinner. Lettuce? Really? That's so . . . healthy. That said, every dude I have made this salad for (even the most dudeliest of dudes) has absolutely loved it. Not only do they love it, but they devour it, lick the bowl, ask me how to make it, text me later asking me again how to make it, and when they see me next, they speak of how they fondly remember that time I made them salad. True story. The moral of the story is: Add BBQ sauce and win the ~~hearts~~ stomachs of dudes.

Prep time: 10 mins (+ 5 mins for the BBQ sauce) • Cook time: 10 mins
Serves: 4-6 as a side, 2-3 as a main

FOR THE SALAD

1 can (19 oz) of chickpeas, drained and rinsed (about 2 cups)

½ cup My Favorite BBQ Sauce (page 209) or store-bought

2 romaine hearts, loosely chopped (about 2 cups)

1 cup cherry tomatoes, sliced in half

½ cucumber, sliced

1 cup cooked corn kernels (thawed frozen works fine)

Several thin slices of red onion (optional)

Lime wedges for garnish

FOR THE RANCH DRESSING

½ cup Mayonnaise for Days (page 208) or store-bought vegan mayo

3 Tbsp non-dairy milk (such as soy or almond)

2 tsp apple cider vinegar

1 tsp dried parsley

1 tsp dried chives

½ tsp onion powder

½ tsp dried dill

¼ tsp garlic powder

¼ tsp salt

1. For the salad, place the chickpeas in a saucepan with the BBQ sauce and put it over medium heat. Let the chickpeas simmer in the sauce for 5–10 minutes, until the sauce thickens and sticks to the chickpeas. Remove from the heat.

2. For the dressing, place all of the dressing ingredients in a small bowl and mix together.

3. Assemble all the salad ingredients, except the lime wedges, in a couple bowls if serving as a main. I like to divide things into sections so it's pretty. Drizzle with the dressing to taste and garnish with wedges of lime. Store leftover dressing in an airtight container in the fridge.

QUICK & EASY PHO

Traditional pho is made from beef broth and can take as long as a day to make. Those are also the two things I don't like about it. This pho is my sneaky-deaky way of pulling this recipe together at lightning-fast speed, just 30 minutes! I've served this to many people—vegans, non-vegans, pho experts—and each and every one of them says exactly the same thing: "Ohmygawd-slurp-thisis-slurp-sogood!"

Prep time: 5 mins • Cook time: 30 mins • Serves: 6

FOR THE BROTH

8 ½ cups vegetable broth

3 cups water

1 yellow onion, quartered

4 cloves garlic, roughly chopped

3 whole star anise

3 whole cloves (the spice)

1-inch piece fresh ginger, peeled and sliced into coins

1 cinnamon stick

Soy sauce to taste (gluten-free, if preferred)

1 package (14 oz) wide rice noodles

1. Place the broth, water, onion, garlic, star anise, whole cloves, ginger, and cinnamon in a large saucepan and bring to a simmer over medium heat. Cover and let simmer for 20–30 minutes, until fragrant and totally scrumptious. Taste and add soy sauce as needed. The amount you need will vary a bit depending on your taste preference and how salty the broth is.

2. While it simmers, clean and chop your toppings. You can use whatever combination you like.

3. Bring a big pot of water to a boil and cook your rice noodles according to the package directions. Drain and then rinse with cold water to stop the noodles cooking.

4. When everything is ready, serve by placing the noodles in individual bowls. Use a ladle to collect the broth, leaving the onions and spices behind. Pile on the toppings to taste.

•••••••••• Cool Tip ••••••••••

This broth gets even more flavorful the next day, so feel free to make this recipe ahead of time, and store leftovers in the fridge in an airtight container for up to a week.

MY FAVE TOPPINGS

Fresh basil (Thai basil is preferable if you can find it) • Cilantro • Fresh mint • Green onions • Mung bean sprouts • Hot peppers (I like mirasol peppers, which are long, red, and not very spicy) • Peanuts • Sautéed mushrooms (I like shiitakes) • Sautéed tofu • Hot sauce • Lime wedges

CREAMY DREAMY COLESLAW

You know that fluorescent green "coleslaw" you see in grocery stores and gross restaurants? (Yes, I'm totally judging.) That stuff doesn't even deserve to be called coleslaw. In fact, it brings shame to the coleslaw name. When people tell me they don't like coleslaw, I know that they must be referring to *that* atrocity. *This* coleslaw is REAL coleslaw. A thing of beauty—crunchy, colorful, creamy, slightly sweet, and tangy. Have this as a side, or dude, seriously, heap this on that Epic BBQ Black Bean Sandwich (page 105), and prepare for a total mouth explosion.

Prep time: 15 mins (+ 5 mins for the mayonnaise) • Serves: 8

FOR THE SLAW

3 cups finely sliced green cabbage

3 cups finely sliced red cabbage

3 medium carrots, cut into match-sticks

8 green onions, chopped

1 cup raisins or dried cranberries

½ cup sliced almonds

FOR THE DRESSING

½ cup Mayonnaise for Days (page 208) or store-bought

2 Tbsp apple cider vinegar

1 Tbsp Dijon mustard (check for gluten-free, if necessary)

1 Tbsp agave or maple syrup

1 tsp onion powder

1 tsp celery seed

1. For the slaw, place the green and red cabbage, carrots, green onions, and raisins in a large bowl.

2. For the dressing, mix all the dressing ingredients together in a small bowl.

3. To the slaw, add dressing to taste, and toss well to combine. This salad gets even better if it sits for a bit, so feel free to make it ahead and store in the fridge overnight or until ready to serve. Sprinkle the almonds over top right before you eat so that they're at peak fresh crunchiness. Store leftover dressing in an airtight container in the fridge.

• • • • • • • • • • • • • • Cool Tip • • • • • • • • • • • • • •

If you have a mandolin or slicer blade for your food processor, it will make chopping much easier, and quicker! You can also use a grater.

ALL HAIL CAESAR SALAD

In my opinion, Caesar salad is basically the ultimate comfort food salad. Yes, in my world, salad can be comfort food. (I know, that's soooo vegan of me.) But hear me out: Crispy romaine lettuce, crunchy homemade croutons, creamy cashew Caesar dressing, all topped with coconut bacon bits . . . I know you're feeling me on this one.

Prep time: 10 mins (+ 10 mins for the mayonnaise and the coconut bacon)
Cook time: About 15 mins • Serves: 4

FOR THE CROUTONS

2 Tbsp olive oil

1 Tbsp nutritional yeast

½ tsp garlic powder

¼ tsp salt

2 slices of day-old bread (gluten-free, if preferred), sliced into ½-inch cubes

FOR THE DRESSING

½ cup Mayonnaise for Days (page 208) or store-bought vegan mayo

1 Tbsp fresh lemon juice

1 Tbsp nutritional yeast

1 tsp Dijon mustard

1 clove garlic, finely minced

1 tsp capers, finely minced

¼ tsp salt

FOR THE SALAD

2 romaine hearts, loosely chopped

1 recipe Addictive Coconut Bacon Bits (page 210)

1. To make the croutons, preheat your oven to 350°F.

2. For the croutons, in a large bowl, mix together the olive oil, nutritional yeast, garlic powder, and salt. Add the bread cubes to the bowl and toss well so they're evenly coated in the olive oil mixture. I find this easiest to do with my hands. Spread the croutons in a single layer on a rimmed baking sheet. Bake for 12–15 minutes, until the croutons are golden and crispy, checking on them often so they don't burn.

3. To make the dressing, place all the dressing ingredients in a bowl and mix together.

4. To assemble the salad, place the romaine hearts and croutons in a large bowl. Add dressing to taste and toss well to combine. Sprinkle the coconut bacon over top. Store any leftover dressing in an airtight container in the fridge.

• • • • • • • • • • • • • • •   Cool Tip   • • • • • • • • • • • • • • •

I love coconut bacon bits in this salad, but feel free to sub chopped up Insanely Good Rice Paper Bacon (page 26) if you're feeling that vibe instead.

GET WELL SOON NOODLE SOUP

Got a cold or the flu? This is the soup for you. But here's a little secret: I eat this soup whether I'm sick or not. I can whip it up with ingredients I usually have on hand, it's easy on the tummy and perfect on the taste buds, and there's even a little pasta goodness—can you go wrong? I think not. The tofu adds a nice chew to this soup, but if tofu ain't your thang, or you just don't have it on hand, it's great without it as well.

 GLUTEN-FREE

Prep time: 10 mins • Cook time: 30 mins • Serves: 8

1 Tbsp olive oil

½ block (6 oz) extra-firm tofu, cut into ½-inch cubes (optional)

2 medium carrots, peeled and sliced

2 stalks celery, sliced

2 cloves garlic, minced

½ yellow onion, chopped

1 bay leaf

½ tsp dried thyme leaves

8 cups low-sodium vegetable broth

2 cups wheat or gluten-free pasta (I like angel hair broken into short pieces, bowties, penne, or macaroni)

¼–½ tsp salt

¼ tsp black pepper

1. Heat the olive oil over medium heat in a large saucepan. Add the tofu (if using), carrots, celery, garlic, onion, bay leaf, and thyme. Sauté until the onion has softened and everything begins to brown and become very fragrant, about 10 minutes.

2. Stir in the broth and use your spoon to scrape the bottom of the saucepan to release any flavorful bits that are stuck there. Add the pasta and bring to a simmer, cover, and cook for about 10 minutes until the soup is hot and delicious. Add in the pasta and cook another 5–10 minutes (depending on the type of pasta you opt for) until noodles are al dente. Season with salt and pepper to taste.

• • • • • • • • • • • • • • •   Cool Tip   • • • • • • • • • • • • • • •

I recommend using a low-sodium vegetable broth for at least half of the vegetable broth used in this recipe; I find most vegetable broths are too salty. You can always add more salt to taste, if you feel it needs it.

GOT A COLD OR FLU?

THIS SOUP IS FOR YOU!

LOVE LETTER FRENCH ONION SOUP

If I had to write a love letter to a vegetable, it would be to the onion.

Dear Onion,

How I love thee. You woo me with your sweet side, you tease me with your spicy side. How I can't wait to peel all those layers off...

xo,
Sam

Ok, enough of that. You get my point. Onions and I are tight. So, when I make this French onion soup, you know I am in love! . . . With onions.

 Prep time: 10 mins • **Cook time:** 45-50 mins (+ 7 mins for the mozzarella)
Serves: 8-10

3 Tbsp olive oil

5 yellow onions, thinly sliced

2 cloves garlic, minced

1–1 ½ tsp salt

¼ tsp white sugar

3 Tbsp all-purpose flour (or gluten-free all-purpose flour blend)

8 cups vegetable broth

½ cup white wine or white vermouth

2 bay leaves

½ tsp black pepper

8–10 slices of baguette (gluten-free, if preferred)

Double recipe of Life-Changing Mozzarella (page 200)

1. Heat the olive oil in a large saucepan over medium heat, then add the onions and garlic. Cover and cook for 15 minutes, stirring and adjusting the heat as needed to make sure they don't burn. Remove the lid, and stir in the salt and sugar. Cook, uncovered and stirring often, until the onions have browned nicely, 5–10 minutes more.

2. When the onions are brown, stir in the flour, and cook for another couple minutes, until the flour has turned to a paste. Do not let it burn. Now stir in the broth, white wine, bay leaves, and pepper. Use your spoon to scrape the bottom of the saucepan to release any flavorful bits that are stuck there. Simmer, covered, on low, for about 20 minutes.

3. In the meantime, toast the baguette slices. Remove and discard the bay leaves from the soup. Divide the soup among oven-safe bowls, top each with a slice of toast, letting it sink into the broth, then spoon the mozzarella over top. Put the bowls on a baking sheet so they're easier to handle, then put them under the broiler until the cheese is bubbly and lightly browned on the top, 2–5 minutes. Keep a close eye on them to make sure they don't burn! Enjoy hot and melty.

EDAMAME & MANDARIN ORANGE MONSTER SALAD

This is a total Eat the Rainbow Salad. Jam-packed with every color, it just screams nutrition. I can never get enough of monster salads like this. Tangy sesame ginger dressing drizzled over an explosion of veggie goodness topped with sweet mandarin oranges and crispy almond slices makes for the most scrumptious of salads. I could eat this all day long.

Prep time: 15 mins • Serves: 4

FOR THE SESAME GINGER DRESSING

⅓ cup rice vinegar

3 cloves garlic, minced

1-inch piece fresh ginger, peeled and minced

1 Tbsp agave

1 Tbsp sesame seeds, plus more for garnish

2 tsp sesame oil

FOR THE SALAD

1 romaine heart, chopped

2 cups finely sliced red cabbage,

2 medium carrots, cut into match-sticks

½ cup cooked edamame (thawed frozen edamame work great)

2 green onions, chopped

½ cup cilantro, roughly chopped

½ cup mandarin orange segments

¼ cup sliced almonds

1. For the dressing, mix all the ingredients together in a small bowl.

2. For the salad, place all the salad ingredients in a large bowl and toss well to combine. Dress to taste and garnish with some sesame seeds. Store leftover dressing in an airtight container in the fridge.

ABSURDLY CHEESY BROCCOLI SOUP

I made this soup on a whim and just guessed at what might make it cheesy. OMG, I totally nailed this on the first go and was actually shocked by how insanely delicious it turned out. The scrumptious cheesiness in this soup come from my ol' fiber-packed friend the potato and my favorite creamy nuts, cashews, making this a much healthier alternative than the traditional version, but without losing any of the flavor.

 GLUTEN-FREE Prep time: 10 mins • Cook time: 35 mins • Serves: 6-8

1 Tbsp olive oil

1 yellow onion, chopped

4 cloves garlic, minced

3 cups peeled and cubed russet potatoes (about 2–3 potatoes)

1 cup raw cashews

4 cups vegetable broth

2 cups water

1 head of broccoli, cut into florets (about 5 cups)

¼ cup nutritional yeast

½ tsp sweet paprika

¼ tsp ground turmeric

½–1 tsp salt

¼ tsp black pepper

1. Heat the olive oil in a large saucepan over medium-high heat. Sauté the onion and garlic for about 5 minutes, until the onion softens and begins to brown.

2. Add the potato and cashews to the saucepan and then add the broth and water. Use a spoon to scrape the bottom of the pan to get any flavorful bits off the bottom. Bring to a boil, then turn down the heat to medium-low to simmer, covered, for about 15 minutes, until the potatoes are completely cooked and the cashews are tender.

3. Blend the soup until completely smooth with an immersion blender or in a powerful standing blender. If you're using a standing blender, blend small batches of the soup at a time, leaving lots of room in the blender so that the hot soup doesn't erupt out the top. Return the blended soup to the saucepan.

4. Add the broccoli, nutritional yeast, paprika, and turmeric to the soup. Cook for an additional 10–15 minutes until the broccoli is tender. Season with salt and pepper to taste.

•••••••• Cool Tip ••••••••

For a lightened-up version, scratch the cashews and use an additional russet potato.

SMOKY TOMATO BASIL CREAM SOUP

This soup tastes super-gourmet, but it is so easy to make. There is something about adding a dash of smoke to tomato soup that really takes it from ordinary lunch item to wow-this-is-so-fancy luncheon course!

Prep time: 5 mins (+ 5 mins for the heavy cream) • Cook time: 25 mins
Serves: 4-6

1 Tbsp olive oil

1 yellow onion, chopped

3 cloves garlic, minced

1 can (28 oz) crushed tomatoes

2 cups vegetable broth

1 small bunch basil leaves (reserve some for garnish)

¼ tsp liquid smoke

¾ cup Heavenly Heavy Cream (page 206)

2 tsp white sugar

¼ tsp salt

¼ tsp black pepper

•••••••••• Cool Tip ••••••••••

For a more traditional tomato basil cream soup, simply omit the liquid smoke.

1. Heat the olive oil in a large saucepan over medium heat. Add the onion and garlic. Sauté for about 5 minutes, until the onion softens and begins to brown.

2. Add the tomatoes, vegetable broth, basil leaves, and liquid smoke. Bring to a simmer, cover, and cook for about 20 minutes, until the tomato is cooked.

3. Use an immersion blender to blend everything together until creamy and smooth. If you want to use a standing blender, blend the soup in small batches, being careful not to fill the blender too high, so soup doesn't explode out the top.

4. Return the soup to the saucepan over medium heat, and stir in the Heavenly Heavy Cream, sugar, salt, and pepper. Serve hot, garnished with a couple basil leaves, a drizzle of Heavenly Heavy Cream, and served with a side of crusty bread. Or, better yet, make my grilled cheese sandwich (page 99) and dunk it straight into the soup.

BURGERS & SANDWICHES

I've never really been a fan of sandwiches, and hamburgers always made me sick. Like, really. There was something about hamburgers that made my stomach groan in pain whenever I ate them. Then a magical thing happened. I went vegan, and now burgers are one of my favorite meals! True story. Just ask my mom. I also gained a new love and appreciation for sandwiches— and all those layers of flavors and textures. I had been doing sandwiches all wrong. I'm happy to say that I'm doing them very, very right now.

T.L.T. (TEMPEH OR TOFU, LETTUCE, ¿ TOMATO)

Do you have half a block of leftover tofu or tempeh? Or perhaps you just want to have some sandwich toppers ready to go on the fry-up when the sandwich mood strikes. I love making these strips—and the longer they marinate, the more flavorful they get! I leave them hanging out in my fridge for up to a week, and then when a sandwich mood strikes, I heat up a pan, crisp them up, and then layer them on my sandwich. They're smoky, salty, slightly sweet, and delightfully chewy. Yus puh-lease!

Prep time: 10 mins (+ 10 mins to overnight to marinate + 5 mins for the mayonnaise) • Cook time: 10 mins • Makes: 2 sandwiches

FOR THE TEMPEH OR TOFU

2 Tbsp maple syrup or agave

1 Tbsp soy sauce (gluten-free, if preferred)

1 Tbsp olive oil, plus more for frying

1 tsp liquid smoke

¼ tsp garlic powder

¼ tsp sweet paprika

½ block (8 oz) tempeh or ½ block (6 oz) extra-firm tofu, thinly sliced

TO ASSEMBLE

4 slices of bread or 2 tortillas (gluten-free, if preferred)

Mayonnaise for Days (page 208) or store-bought vegan mayo

A few lettuce leaves

Several slices of tomato

1. In a bowl or large resealable plastic bag, mix together the maple syrup, soy sauce, olive oil, liquid smoke, garlic powder, and paprika. Add the tempeh or tofu to this marinade and let it soak for about 10 minutes, or as long as a week.

2. Heat some olive oil in a frying pan and fry the tempeh or tofu for about 5 minutes per side, or until browned and crispy. As the strips cook, keep spooning the leftover marinade on top until you run out. The marinade will turn into a sticky glaze that will make it all taste extra amazing!

3. To serve, spread a slice of bread or tortilla with vegan mayonnaise and top with lettuce, tomato, and the tempeh or tofu slices. Devour.

• • • • • • • • • • • • • • •   Amper-Uppers   • • • • • • • • • • • • • •

Add some avocado slices to take this sandwich up a notch, and make it a T.L.A.T.

BOSS BBQ VEGGIE BURGER

The veggie burgers in the store are fine . . . I guess . . . but I find them thin, boring, and very processed. And homemade veggie burgers are great, but often aren't able to hold up on the grill. This was a serious problem I needed to solve, and it wasn't easy. After many, many, MANY tests, techniques, and failed attempts, I finally nailed it. I present to you a homemade veggie burger that is strong enough for the grill, easy enough to whip up in just 20 minutes, and packs some serious BBQ punch.

Prep time: 10 mins • Cook time: 10 mins (+40 mins for the brown rice)
Makes: 8 large or 14 extra-thin patties

2 Tbsp ground chia or flax seeds

¼ cup warm water

1 can (19 oz) black beans, drained and rinsed (about 2 cups)

2 cups cooked brown rice

1 cup walnuts, finely chopped

1 cup panko bread crumbs (or gluten-free bread crumbs)

½ cup all-purpose flour (or gluten-free all-purpose flour blend)

6 cloves garlic, minced

1 yellow onion, chopped

2 Tbsp smooth natural peanut butter

4 tsp smoked paprika

4 tsp chili powder

1 tsp salt

1 tsp black pepper

1. In a small bowl, mix the chia seeds into the water, then transfer to a food processor and add all the other ingredients. Pulse several times to combine until the mixture holds together when pinched, but you can still see some texture. Form 8 thick patties or about 14 very thin patties. Thick burgers are great for the grill or a hearty burger, while thin patties must be fried and are great for making a double burger (my fave!).

2. To fry the burgers, heat enough oil to cover the bottom of your frying pan over medium heat. Fry the burgers until lightly crisp outside and fully cooked inside, about 5 minutes on each side. Low and slow is the way to go.

3. To grill the burgers, lightly brush the grill with a bit of oil to prevent sticking. Grill for a couple of minutes on each side, until grill marks are formed and the burgers are cooked through. Low and slow here, too.

• • • • • • • • • • • • •   Cool Tip   • • • • • • • • • • • • •

You can freeze the prepared, cooked, and cooled burgers by laying them out in a single layer on a baking sheet and popping in the freezer until completely frozen. Store them together in a bag or container for up to a month. To reheat from frozen, preheat your oven to 375°F and bake for 20-30 minutes, until heated through.

STOLE MY HEART OF PALM ROLL

I love how tender, zesty, and creamy this sandwich is, but also how quick and easy it is to whip up. If you're new to heart of palm, it has a mild, tangy taste similar to artichokes, and has a very cool, almost flaky texture.

Prep time: 10 mins (+ 5 mins for the mayonnaise)
Makes: 2 sandwiches

1 can (14 oz) heart of palm, drained and chopped

2 Tbsp Mayonnaise for Days (page 208) or store-bought vegan mayo

1 tsp fresh lemon juice

1 tsp capers, chopped

¼ tsp salt

¼ tsp black pepper

1 stalk celery, finely chopped

½ yellow or red onion, finely chopped

2 bread rolls (gluten-free, if preferred)

1. Toss the hearts of palm, mayonnaise, lemon juice, capers, salt, and pepper into a large bowl. Use a fork or potato masher to smash the heart of palm into smaller pieces, but try to leave some texture.

2. Add the celery and red onion and stir to incorporate. Fill the bread rolls with filling, and enjoy your new fave sandwich.

•••••••••••••••••• Vegan Tidbit ••••••••••••••••••

If you're concerned about the sustainability of heart of palm, rest assured that, unlike some palm oils, most canned variety of this veggie comes from farmed peach palms. But, if you'd like to avoid using heart of palm, artichoke hearts are a good substitution. The flavor will be a little different, but it'll still make for a tasty sandwich.

GO-TO CHICKPEA SALAD SANDWICH

This is hands down my favorite sandwich, and it's my vegan answer to a tuna or chicken salad sandwich. It's super easy to make, tastes great, and I almost always have all the ingredients in my pantry and fridge. You can enjoy as-is, or you can layer on some extra veggies. This is such a classic in my house that you'll often find me forking at leftovers straight from the fridge.

Prep time: 10 mins (+ 5 mins for the mayonnaise)
Makes: 4 sandwiches

1 can (19 oz) chickpeas, drained and rinsed (about 2 cups)

3 Tbsp Mayonnaise for Days (page 208) or store-bought vegan mayo

1 Tbsp Dijon mustard (check for gluten-free, if necessary)

2 tsp capers (optional)

¼ tsp salt

¼ tsp black pepper

2 stalks celery, chopped

¼ red onion, chopped

8 slices of bread or 4 tortillas (gluten-free, if preferred)

1. Toss the chickpeas, mayonnaise, mustard, capers, salt, and pepper into a food processor and pulse to combine until the chickpeas reach a nice mashed texture, but not puréed. Alternatively, you could do this with a fork or potato masher if you don't have a food processor. Add the celery and red onion and pulse a few more times just to incorporate, or stir to mix in.

2. Pile on top of bread or a tortilla. Top with extra veggies of your choice if you wish.

Grilled cheeses can be made sweet or savory, and the combinations are endless.

GET CREATIVE!

THE ART OF THE PERFECT VEGAN GRILLED CHEESE SANDWICH

Yes, it is an art. If you want a grilled cheese sandwich that is gorgeous enough to hang on your wall (although I really don't recommend that), this is for you. I have a sneaky trick up my sleeve that will make your grilled chees perfectly cheesy and gooey! (Keep reading!)

Prep time: 5 mins • Cook time: About 10 mins per sandwich (+ 7 mins for the mozzarella) • Makes: 4 sandwiches

2 Tbsp vegan butter

8 slices of bread (gluten-free, if preferred)

1 recipe Life-Changing Mozzarella (page 200) or 1 recipe Nacho Cheese Love (page 201) (or both!)

1. Butter both sides of the bread. Heat a frying pan over medium-low heat. Place two slices of the buttered bread in the pan and cook for a few minutes, until the sides facing down are golden and toasty.

2. Remove one slice from the pan and flip the other over so the toasted side is facing up. Dollop on the cheese and any additional toppings you like, then top with the other side of bread, toasted side down, and continue to cook until the sandwich is golden on the edges and the cheese is hot and melty, about 3 minutes.

3. Use your spatula to lightly press the edges together to help form a seal. When the bottom is nicely toasted, flip and cook the sandwich on the other side until both sides are toasted and the sandwich is warm all the way through, about 3 minutes on each side.

-CHEESY ADDITIONS-

Onions • Caramelized onions •Tomato • Apple slices, fig slices, pear slices, or strawberries • Hot peppers • Avocado • Basil or other fresh herbs • Pickles • Sautéed mushrooms • Vegan pesto • Tempeh or tofu (as prepared on page 90) • Addictive Coconut Bacon Bits (page 210) • Insanely Good Rice Paper Bacon (page 26) • Jams or chutneys • Roasted vegetables

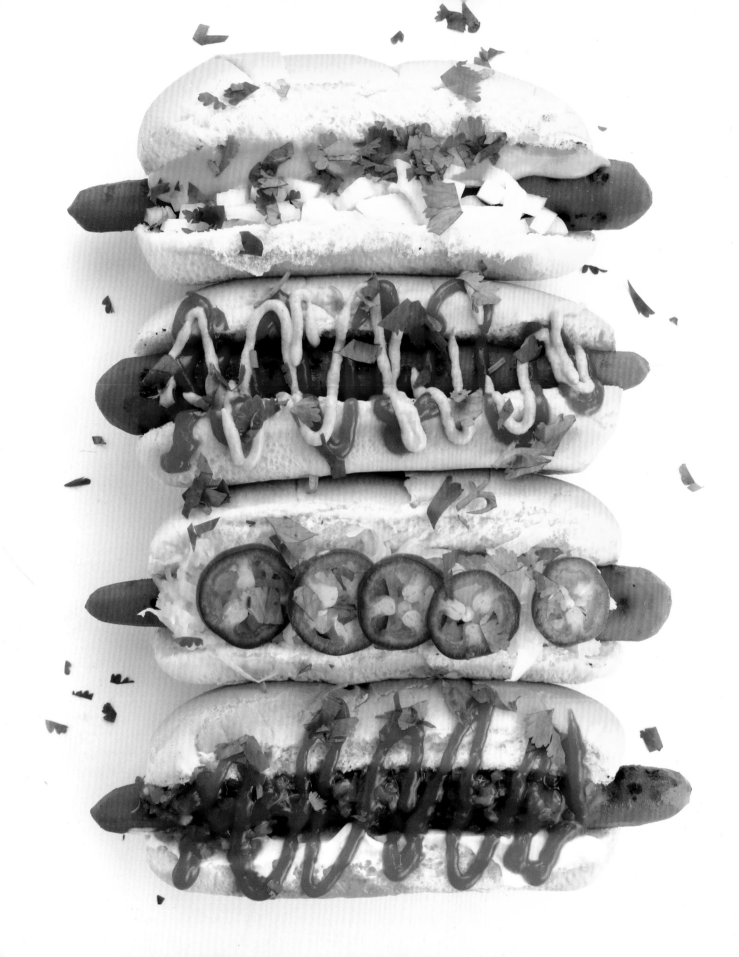

CARROT DOGS ARE TOTALLY A THING!

These days, almost any grocery store will have veggie dogs in stock, and those are a totally great quick grab on your way to a friend's BBQ. But, if you're looking for a healthier version that tastes even better, you must try these carrot dogs! They're surprisingly delicious and easy to make. Top with all your favorite toppings and be prepared to be blown away (yes, by a carrot).

Prep time: 5 mins (+ overnight to marinate, if desired)
Cook time: 20 mins • Makes: 4-6 carrot dogs

4–6 veggie dog–sized carrots
(as many as can fit in a single layer
in your pan)

2 cups water

3 Tbsp soy sauce (gluten-free,
if preferred)

1 tsp smoked paprika

½ tsp garlic powder

½ tsp onion powder

½ tsp dried mustard

¼ tsp black pepper

4–6 hot dog buns (gluten-free,
if preferred)

Toppings of choice

•••••••• Cool Tip ••••••••

These are great for making ahead of time, as they get more flavorful the longer they sit in the marinade, up to 2 days.

1. Cut off the tops of the carrots, then peel the carrots. If you like, you can use your peeler to shape the ends to round them out a bit and make the carrots look more like veggie dogs.

2. In a saucepan just wide enough to fit the carrots, place the water, soy sauce, paprika, garlic powder, onion powder, dried mustard, and pepper. Whisk together, then add the carrots, laying them in a single layer. Bring to a simmer over medium heat and cook for 10–15 minutes, until the carrots are fork tender but not mushy. It's fine if the carrots aren't completely submerged; just turn them a few times as they cook.

3. You can use the carrots right away, but they're even better if you let them cool in their marinade, then put the saucepan in the fridge, or transfer them to an airtight container along with all the cooking liquid, so the carrots can marinate overnight, or for up to 2 days.

4. You can grill or pan-fry the carrot dogs. To grill them, just toss the carrots on a hot BBQ and turn as needed until they're grilled all the way around, about 5 minutes. To pan-fry them, add a bit of oil to a frying pan and put it over medium-high heat. Fry until browned on each side, about 5 minutes.

5. Serve on a bun and garnish as you would your favorite veggie dog. Ketchup, Mayonnaise for Days (page 208), mustard, pickles, onions, whatever you fancy.

STAY-HOME PHILLY CHEESE MUSHROOM SANDWICH

In my pre-vegan days, I went to Philly and had their world-famous sandwich. I have to say, I was truly disappointed. It was so greasy and completely lacking in flavor. But even though it was unremarkable and bland, I still liked the concept of the sandwich and was inspired to create my own vegan version. Mine turned out light years better than the original: Juicy, cheesy, hearty, flavor-packed, and no traveling to Philly required.

Prep time: 10 mins • Cook time: 10 mins (+ 7 mins for the mozzarella)
Makes: 2 heaping sandwiches

1 Tbsp olive oil

1 yellow onion, thinly sliced

1 red or green bell pepper, thinly sliced

16 oz mushrooms of choice, thickly sliced (about 3 cups)

2 cloves garlic, minced

½–1 jalapeño pepper, thinly sliced

¼ tsp liquid smoke

¼ tsp salt

2 bread rolls (gluten-free, if preferred)

½ recipe Life-Changing Mozzarella (page 200), warmed

¼ cup cilantro, roughly chopped

1. Heat the olive oil in a frying pan over medium-low heat. Add the onion and bell pepper. Slowly cook until the onion and pepper begin to soften, about 5 minutes.

2. Add the mushrooms, garlic, jalapeño (as much or as little as you like depending on your spice preference), liquid smoke, and salt. Cover and continue to cook for about 5 minutes more, stirring every now and then until the mushrooms are cooked and the onions have caramelized.

3. Pile the cooked mushrooms high on the bread rolls, top with several dollops of mozzarella, and garnish with cilantro.

EPIC BBQ BLACK BEAN SANDWICH

If you've never had beans on a sandwich before, my guess is you will want to from now on. Hearty, flavorful, sauce dripping down your arm, this sandwich is everything a good hot sandwich should be, and takes only 15 minutes to make. If you want to make this sandwich even more epic, top it with a big scoop of Creamy Dreamy Coleslaw (page 75).

Prep time: 5 mins (+ 15 mins for the coleslaw + 5 mins for the BBQ sauce) • Cook time: 10 mins • Makes: 4 sandwiches

1 Tbsp olive oil

½ yellow onion, finely chopped

2 cloves garlic, minced

1 can (19 oz) black beans drained and rinsed (about 2 cups)

¼ cup My Favorite BBQ Sauce (page 209) or store-bought vegan BBQ sauce

8 slices of bread, 4 burger buns, or 4 tortillas (gluten-free, if preferred)

Creamy Dreamy Coleslaw (page 75)

1. Heat a frying pan over medium-high heat and add the olive oil. Toss in the onion and garlic and sauté for about 5 minutes, until the onion softens and begins to brown.

2. Stir in the black beans and BBQ sauce. Cook for another 5 minutes, until everything is heated through.

3. Pile the beans on bread, buns, or tortillas, then drizzle a little extra BBQ sauce on top. Top with a big scoop of coleslaw.

CREAMY COCONUT MUSHROOMS ON TOAST

This is one of my go-to, lazy-night, need-something-creamy-and-satisfying-immediately dinners. This gorgeous open-faced sandwich is one that you eat with a fork and knife (makes me feel so fancy). A lovely crusty bread is ideal for this, but the mushrooms are so sinfully creamy that any bread will do.

Prep time: 5 mins • Cook time: 10 mins • Makes: 4 open-faced sandwiches

1 Tbsp coconut oil (sub any oil or vegan butter if needed)

16 oz button mushrooms, sliced (about 3 cups)

4 cloves garlic, minced

⅓ cup full-fat coconut milk, plus more as needed

1 Tbsp nutritional yeast

½ tsp dried thyme leaves

½ tsp dried oregano

¼ tsp salt

¼ tsp black pepper

4 slices of bread, toasted (gluten-free, if preferred)

2 Tbsp cilantro or parsley, chopped

1. Heat the oil in a frying pan over medium-high heat. Add the mushrooms and garlic and sauté for about 5 minutes, until the mushrooms soften and begin to release their juices.

2. Turn down the heat to a simmer, and stir in the coconut milk, nutritional yeast, thyme, oregano, salt, and pepper. Continue to cook for about another 5 minutes, until the coconut milk has reduced a bit. If you want it a bit saucier, add small splashes of coconut milk until your desired sauciness is reached.

3. Divide the mushrooms on top of the toast, then garnish with cilantro and an extra crack of pepper.

FEAST
YOUR EYES
(& BELLY)

Let's get to the real ~~meat~~ veggies of this cookbook.
I love me some big portions of savory goodness. I'm the kind of girl who
will eat leftover stir-fry for breakfast. So, when I say this is hands down
my favorite chapter of this book, I mean it!

This is the part of the book where I prove that you don't need to live off
fake meat alternatives, and you also don't need to live off quinoa and kale.
Now, don't get me wrong, there is nothing wrong with any of those things,
but when I'm hungry, I want Crispy Coconut Cauliflower Tacos (page 117),
15-Minute Peanut Noodles (page 110), a slice (or more) of Caramelized Onion
Pizza to Die For (page 137), or a ginormous bowl of OMG, It's So Good, Tofu
Bolognese (page 115) . . . I'm literally drooling all over this book right now.

15-MINUTE PEANUT NOODLES

Do you like peanut butter? And do you like noodles? You don't!? Then why are you even reading this recipe? Seriously. Ok, never mind. Assuming you *do* like both of those things, you will like this splendidly easy dish. It comes together quickly, and no flavor is sacrificed by the speedy cooking. You can enjoy these noodles hot or cold, making them perfect anytime of the year.

Prep time: 10 mins • Cook time: 5 mins • Serves: 4

FOR THE PEANUT SAUCE

½ cup natural peanut butter (smooth or crunchy)

½ cup water

3 Tbsp soy sauce (gluten-free, if preferred)

2 cloves garlic, minced

2 Tbsp fresh lime juice (1 lime)

1 Tbsp agave or maple syrup

1-inch piece fresh ginger, peeled and minced

2 tsp your favorite hot sauce (optional)

1 tsp sesame oil

FOR THE NOODLES

6 oz vegan chow mein noodles or rice noodles

1 red bell pepper, chopped

1 medium carrot, peeled and cut into matchsticks

2 green onions, chopped

¼ cup peanuts, roughly chopped (salted, roasted, raw, whatever you like!)

Handful of cilantro, roughly chopped

1. For the peanut sauce, in a small bowl, mix together all of the sauce ingredients. Set aside.

2. Cook the noodles according to the package directions. Drain them and return them to the saucepan. Add the peanut sauce, bell pepper, and carrot. Toss well to combine.

3. Garnish with green onions, peanuts, and cilantro. Add more hot sauce if you like.

• • • • • • • • • • • • • Amper-Uppers • • • • • • • • • • • • •

I love the fresh crunch of raw red bell pepper and carrot in this dish, but if you don't happen to have those in your fridge, you could also try chopped cucumber, thinly sliced cabbage, cooked edamame, snow peas, basil leaves, or cubed tofu. This dish is super versatile and a great fridge cleaner-outer.

SPICY BRAISED TOMATO TOFU BURRITO

I lived in California for several years, and it wasn't until Cali that I truly discovered my deep, hidden love called burritos. Sure, I had enjoyed burritos before, but when I began experiencing the huge, flavor bursting, layers of goodness that the burritos were in LA, then I really fell in love.

This juicy, fiery dish is the best tofu burrito filling EVER! Control yourself! You might eat it straight from the pan with a spoon!

Prep time: 10 mins • Cook time: 15 mins • Makes: 4-6 burritos

FOR THE TOFU FILLING

1 Tbsp oil (olive, canola, coconut all work well)

1 onion, chopped

2 cloves garlic, minced

1 block (14 oz) firm or block (12 oz) extra-firm tofu

2 tomatoes, chopped

¼ cup tomato paste

½ lime, juiced

1 Tbsp agave

2 tsp chili powder

2 tsp smoked paprika

1 ½ tsp salt

1 tsp ground cumin

1 tsp crushed red pepper flakes

FOR THE BURRITOS

4–6 large flour tortillas (gluten-free, if preferred)

½ head of lettuce, chopped

1 avocado, chopped

Handful of cilantro, chopped

1. For the tofu filling, place the oil in a frying pan over medium-high heat. Sauté the onion and garlic until softened and beginning to brown, about 5 minutes. Crumble the tofu into the pan, and add all the remaining filling ingredients. Cook until everything is heated through, stirring occasionally, for another 5–7 minutes.

2. Assemble the burritos by scooping some of the tofu mixture onto the tortillas, then topping with lettuce, avocado, and cilantro. Fold both the top and bottom of the tortilla in, then roll it up from the sides so the filling is completely enclosed.

3. Heat a dry frying pan over medium-high heat. Once it's hot, place the burritos seam side down in the pan. Let it toast for a few minutes until golden, and the burrito is sealed closed. Flip and toast the other side until golden. Enjoy!

OMG, IT'S SO GOOD, TOFU BOLOGNESE

In my opinion, pasta is probably one of the world's most perfect foods. I'm pretty sure I could eat it every day and I would still love it. This Bolognese is where it's at—it's chewy, smoky, hearty, and totally lick-the-bowl scrumptious. Just make sure you don't eat all the tofu crumbles before they even make it into the sauce, ok? I've warned you.

Prep time: 5 mins (+ 5 minutes for the parmegan) • Cook time: 35-45 mins (+ 35 minutes for the tomato sauce) • Serves: 4

2 Tbsp nutritional yeast

1 Tbsp soy sauce (gluten-free, if preferred)

1 Tbsp olive oil

1 tsp chili powder

½ tsp garlic powder

¼ tsp liquid smoke (or ½ tsp smoked paprika)

1 block (12 oz) extra-firm tofu

3 cups My Family Favorite Tomato Sauce (page 156), or store-bought

Pasta of choice (gluten-free, if preferred)

Parmegan (page 204), for garnish (optional)

••••••••• Cool Tip ••••••••

You can make the tofu mixture ahead of time and store it in an airtight container in the fridge for up to a week. Just stir it into the hot tomato sauce when you are ready to serve.

1. Preheat your oven to 350°F. Lightly grease a baking pan large enough to hold the tofu without crowding.

2. In a large bowl, mix together the nutritional yeast, soy sauce, olive oil, chili powder, garlic powder, and liquid smoke. This mixture will have a paste-like consistency.

3. Using your fingers, crumble the tofu into the bowl. Mix everything together, making sure all of the tofu is evenly coated. Spread the tofu mixture evenly over the pan and bake for 35–45 minutes, stirring every now and then. Keep a close eye on it toward the end so that it doesn't burn. You want the tofu to be nice and browned. The smaller crumbles will be darker than the larger crumbles, and that's ok because it will provide a variety of texture.

4. Once the tofu is cooked, heat the tomato sauce, and cook the pasta according to the package directions. Stir the tofu into the sauce, and heat through. If you find the sauce is too thick, stir in a bit of water until the desired consistency is reached. Serve over the hot pasta with a sprinkle of Parmegan.

CRISPY COCONUT CAULIFLOWER TACOS

Cauliflower may be boring when it's just steamed or boiled, but there is absolutely nothing boring about these tacos. They taste like summer love to me. Why summer love tastes like crispy coconut cauliflower topped with tangy red onion, cilantro, lime, and sweet mango I have no idea, but damn, it's tasty!

Prep time: 10 mins • Cook time: 30 mins • Makes: 8 tacos

FOR THE CAULIFLOWER

1 cup full-fat coconut milk

1 cup panko bread crumbs

1 cup unsweetened shredded coconut

1 tsp salt

½ tsp garlic powder

½ tsp onion powder

1 cauliflower, cut into florets

FOR THE TACOS

½ red onion

Large handful of cilantro

1 mango

1 lime

8 taco shells, soft or crunchy (gluten-free, if preferred)

•••••• Amper-Uppers ••••••

Drizzle the tacos with a little Avocado Cilantro Sauce (page 141), to kick 'em up a notch.

1. Preheat your oven to 400°F. Line a large baking sheet with parchment paper.

2. For the cauliflower, place the coconut milk in a large bowl. In another large bowl, whisk together the panko, shredded coconut, salt, garlic powder, and onion powder.

3. Take your cauliflower florets and, working in batches, coat them in the coconut milk, then drop them in the panko and shredded coconut mixture. Toss well to coat evenly and then put them on the prepared baking sheet. Bake for 25–30 minutes, flipping halfway through, until the cauliflower is fork tender and the coating is lightly browned.

4. In the meantime, prepare all of your taco ingredients. Thinly slice the red onion, chop the cilantro and mango, and cut the lime into wedges.

5. Assemble the tacos by layering the crispy cauliflower florets with red onion, cilantro, and mango onto taco shells. Finish them off with a squirt of lime juice.

PRO-PINEAPPLE HAWAIIAN PIZZA

I know some of you are anti-pineapple-on-pizza people, but I am on the pro side. Pineapple on pizza was my absolute favorite thing as a kid. The sweet and salty combo just works for me. For this vegan version, I made a simple coconut garlic sauce, which gives the pizza an awesome tropical flavor. Top the whole thing with smoky and chewy tofu bites. . . . Just don't expect me to share this when I make it.

GLUTEN-FREE

Prep time: 5 mins (+ 1 hour 15 mins for the pizza dough)
Cook time: 45-55 mins (+ 35 mins for the tomato sauce) • Makes: 1 large pizza

FOR THE TOFU BITES

½ block (6 oz) extra-firm tofu,
cut into small pieces

1 Tbsp soy sauce (gluten-free,
if preferred)

¼ tsp liquid smoke

FOR THE GARLIC COCONUT SAUCE

1 Tbsp light oil (such as canola or
vegetable)

4 cloves garlic, minced

1 Tbsp flour (any kind)

1 cup full-fat coconut milk

FOR THE PIZZA

1 recipe Go-To Pizza Dough
(page 211) or store-bought (gluten-
free, if preferred)

½ cup My Family Favorite Tomato
Sauce (page 156) or store-bought

1 can (14 oz) pineapple pieces or
rings, drained

1. For the tofu bites, preheat your oven to 325°F and lightly grease a baking pan.

2. Place the tofu pieces in a small bowl, and toss with the soy sauce and liquid smoke. Scatter the tofu with any remaining sauce on the prepared baking pan. Bake for 20–25 minutes, stirring the tofu every now and then, until the bites are dark golden and chewy. Set aside.

3. For the garlic coconut sauce, warm the oil in a medium saucepan over medium heat and then sauté the garlic for just 1 minute, until it just starts to brown. Whisk in the flour and cook another minute. Pour in the coconut milk and whisk well to combine. Bring to a simmer and cook for 2–3 minutes, until slightly thickened. Remove from the heat.

4. For the pizza, increase your oven temperature to 425°F. Lightly grease a pizza pan or baking sheet. Stretch out the dough to fit your sheet. Spread the tomato sauce over the dough, then spread the garlic coconut sauce over top. Sprinkle with the tofu bites and pineapple pieces. Bake for 20–25 minutes, until the crust is golden brown.

RAINBOW PEANUT PINEAPPLE KABOBS

Kabobs are so much fun. They're colorful and grillable, the word "kabob" is fun to say, and these particular ones involve both pineapple and peanut sauce. The key to perfect kabobs is to have an array of different textures and flavors, and a gorgeous sauce to finish them off. I'm smitten with the rainbow of veggies, the chewy tofu, and the sweet, sweet pineapple in this version.

Prep time: 15 mins • Cook time: 15 mins • Makes: 8–10 kabobs

FOR THE PEANUT SAUCE

2 Tbsp natural peanut butter (smooth or crunchy)

1 Tbsp fresh lime juice

1 Tbsp soy sauce (gluten-free, if preferred)

1 Tbsp agave

1-inch piece fresh ginger, peeled and minced

1 clove garlic, minced

FOR THE KABOBS

½ block (6 oz) extra-firm tofu, cut into 1-inch cubes

1 Tbsp soy sauce (gluten-free, if preferred)

1 red bell pepper, cut into 1-inch pieces

1 orange bell pepper, cut into 1-inch pieces

1 zucchini, cut into 1-inch-thick coins, halved

½ red onion, cut into 1-inch pieces

½ pineapple, cut into 1-inch pieces

1. If using wooden skewers, soak them in water for 30 minutes before using so they don't burn.

2. For the peanut sauce, mix all of the sauce ingredients together and set aside.

3. For the kabobs, place the tofu in a bowl with the soy sauce and toss to coat. Thread the tofu, vegetables, and pineapple onto a skewer, leaving a space between each piece and dividing everything evenly between the skewers.

4. Preheat your grill to high. When it's hot, grill the skewers for 10–15 minutes, turning as needed. Remove from the heat and brush with peanut sauce. Serve the remaining sauce on the side for dipping.

BIG OL' BURRITO BOWL

You may notice that us vegans are big fans of giant bowls of things. Some people call them Buddha bowls, but I just call them what they are—big bowls. This big ol' burrito bowl, with its gorgeously seasoned beans, salsa, fresh veggies, and avocado, all on top of a bed of rice, is sure to please any vegan—or non-vegan, for that matter. Don't be scared by the long list of ingredients; it's mainly just spices for the beans. Trust me, all those spices are worth the effort!

Prep time: 10 mins (+ 5 mins for the dressing)
Cook time: 10 mins (+20-40 mins for the rice) • Serves: 4-6

FOR THE BEANS

1 Tbsp oil (olive, canola, coconut all work well)

1 yellow onion, chopped

2 cloves garlic, minced

1 can (19 oz) kidney beans or black beans, drained and rinsed (about 2 cups)

½ cup water

2 tsp molasses, brown sugar, or agave

2 tsp chili powder

1 tsp ground cumin

½ tsp salt

½ tsp smoked paprika

½ tsp dried oregano

½ tsp crushed red pepper flakes (optional, for some spice)

FOR THE BOWL

1 cup salsa

4 cups cooked rice (brown or white)

1 romaine heart, chopped

2 tomatoes, chopped

2 cups cooked corn (thawed frozen works great)

1 avocado, chopped

1 recipe Ranch Dressing (page 70) or Avocado Cilantro Sauce (page 141)

1. For the beans, place the oil in a frying pan over medium-high heat. Sauté the onion and garlic for about 5 minutes, until the onion has softened and is beginning to brown. Add the beans, water, molasses, and all of the spices. Cook for 3 minutes, until heated through and most of the liquid is absorbed, but there's still some sauce.

2. To prepare the bowl, stir the salsa into the cooked rice and heat through.

3. Divide the rice among individual serving bowls, and top with the beans, then lettuce, tomatoes, corn, and avocado. I like to arrange the ingredients so they look pretty. Drizzle the dressing over top to taste.

LIGHTER (: BETTER THAT WAY) CAULIFLOWER FETTUCCINI ALFREDO

It's no secret that traditional Alfredo sauce is jam-packed with fat and calories and pretty much lacking in nutrients. This cauliflower fettuccini Alfredo, on the other hand, is full of cauliflower health but still manages to be delightfully creamy, fulfilling all those sinful pasta cravings. Yep, it is a bit lighter than a traditional Alfredo, but in my opinion that is a good thing, as it doesn't leave you feeling weighed down.

Prep time: 10 mins (+ 10 mins for the heavy cream and parmegan)
Cook time: 10 mins • Serves: 4-6

FOR THE CAULIFLOWER ALFREDO SAUCE

1 cauliflower, roughly chopped

4 cloves garlic, peeled

1 cup vegetable broth

1 cup Heavenly Heavy Cream (page 206) or full-fat coconut milk

2 tsp white miso paste

1 ½ tsp salt

FOR THE PASTA

1 lb fettuccini (gluten-free, if preferred)

Parmegan (page 204)

Handful of parsley, chopped

Black pepper

1. For the cauliflower Alfredo sauce, place the cauliflower, garlic cloves, vegetable broth, and Heavenly Heavy Cream in a large frying pan or saucepan, and bring to a simmer over medium heat. Cook for about 10 minutes, until the cauliflower is very soft and falls apart when pierced with a fork.

2. Add the white miso paste and salt. Using an immersion or stand blender, blend the cauliflower and its cooking liquid. If you use a stand blender, do this in batches, being careful not to fill the blender too high, so the hot liquid doesn't explode out the top.

3. In the meantime, cook the pasta according to the package directions, then drain.

4. Return the pasta to the pan, then pour the cauliflower Alfredo sauce over top. Toss to heat through. To serve, garnish with a sprinkle of Parmegan and parsley, and freshly cracked black pepper.

•••••••• Cool Tip ••••••••

For an even lighter version, swap the Heavenly Heavy Cream or coconut milk with your favorite non-dairy milk.

SCRUMPTIOUS SUN-DRIED TOMATO & WALNUT BEAN BALLS

One of my pet peeves when it comes to many homemade bean balls is that they fall apart when stabbed with a fork. So, for this cookbook, I was absolutely determined to make a bean ball that was fork-proof. And, success! Not only are they stabbable, but these bean balls have some seriously drool-worthy goodness. Add these bad boys to a monster bowl of pasta with My Family Favorite Tomato Sauce (page 156) or serve them as an appetizer with warm My Favorite BBQ Sauce (page 209) for dipping. You won't regret it.

 GLUTEN-FREE   Prep time: 15 mins • Cook time: 25 mins • Makes: About 20 bean balls

1 Tbsp ground chia or flax seeds

2 ½ Tbsp warm water

1 cup canned or cooked kidney beans, drained and rinsed

1 cup cooked brown rice

½ yellow onion, chopped

½ cup dried bread crumbs (gluten-free, if preferred)

½ cup roughly chopped walnuts

¼ cup all-purpose flour (or gluten-free all-purpose flour blend)

¼ cup sun-dried tomatoes (the dry kind, not in oil), chopped

4 cloves garlic, minced

2 tsp dried basil

½ tsp salt

½ tsp black pepper

1. Mix the chia seeds into the water and set aside to thicken, about 5–10 minutes.

2. Add the thickened chia to a food processor with all the other ingredients except the oil, and pulse until the mixture comes together but still has texture. Don't turn it to mush! You can test that it's blended properly by trying to form a ball. If the ball holds together, it's good to go. If not, pulse a few more times. Form the mixture into 2-inch balls.

3. To fry the bean balls (my fave!), place the oil in a frying pan and put it over medium heat. Slowly fry the bean balls in batches, making sure to turn them so they brown evenly on all sides. Remove the balls from the pan and drain them on paper towel.

4. To bake the bean balls, preheat your oven to 350°F. Lightly grease a rimmed baking sheet. Bake, shaking the pan every now and then, until the bean balls are golden brown on all sides and feel firm when pressed, 20–25 minutes.

ROASTED BUTTERNUT SQUASH & PURPLE SLAW TACOS

Have you ever heard of squash and purple slaw tacos? Me neither! That's exactly why I had to make these beauties. They're super pretty, and super-DUPER delicious. This dish is a work of art—not only looks-wise but also flavor-wise.

STANDARD TACO FILLING:
Brown and boring. BOO!

THIS TACO FILLING:
Colorful and exciting. YAY!

GLUTEN-FREE

Prep time: 10 mins • Cook time: 30 mins • Makes: 8 tacos

FOR THE BUTTERNUT SQUASH

3 ½ cups butternut squash, peeled and cut into 1-inch cubes

1 Tbsp olive oil

¼ tsp salt

FOR THE PURPLE SLAW

¼ red cabbage, shredded

Handful of cilantro, roughly chopped

2 Tbsp fresh lime juice (1 lime)

2 tsp agave

¼ tsp crushed red pepper flakes

¼ tsp salt

FOR THE TACOS

8 taco shells, soft or crunchy (gluten-free, if preferred)

Your favorite hot sauce

1. For the butternut squash, preheat your oven to 400°F.

2. Spread the butternut squash cubes on a rimmed baking sheet, drizzle with the oil, and sprinkle with the salt. Stir to evenly coat all the cubes. Bake for 25–30 minutes, until cooked through and browned on the edges.

3. Meanwhile, for the purple slaw, mix all the slaw ingredients together and set aside. It will get even more flavorful and tender as it sits.

4. To assemble the tacos, turn down the oven temperature to 350°F. If using the soft tortillas, wrap them in foil and heat in the oven for about 10 minutes, until warmed through. The crunchy shells can be heated according to package directions. Scoop some butternut squash and some slaw onto each tortilla, then top with your favorite hot sauce.

SUH-WEET POTATO POT PIE

Chicken pot pie, schmicken pot pie. We all know the reason people say a dish "tastes like chicken" is because chicken is boooorinnggg and just takes on the flavors of what's around it. The best flavor from a chicken pot pie comes from all the glorious veggies. So, let's cut out the middle man, get to the good stuff, and make a veggie-packed pot pie. In my opinion, one of the kings of the delicious veggie world is the sweet potato. It takes this pot pie from yum to YU-UM! And I guarantee that it definitely doesn't taste like chicken. ~Wink wink~

Prep time: 10 mins (+ 15 mins for the pie crust) • Cook time: 40 mins • Serves: 6-8

1 Tbsp olive oil

3 medium carrots, peeled and cut into 1-inch cubes

3 cloves garlic, minced

2 sweet potatoes, peeled and cut into 1-inch cubes

1 onion, chopped

6 Tbsp all-purpose flour

3 cups vegetable broth

1 tsp dried thyme leaves

1 tsp salt

½ tsp black pepper

1 cup fresh or frozen peas

½ cup non-dairy milk

1 recipe My Nana's Perfect Pie Crust (page 214) or store-bought vegan deep pie crust

1. Preheat your oven to 375°F.

2. Heat the olive oil in large saucepan over medium-high heat. Add the carrots, garlic, sweet potatoes, and onion. Cover, and cook for 8–12 minutes, stirring often, until the sweet potatoes are fork tender, but not mushy.

3. Remove the lid, then sprinkle the flour across the veggies. Stir to coat the veggies with the flour, and cook for another minute. Pour in the vegetable broth, thyme, salt, and pepper. Mix everything well and cook, uncovered, until the sauce has thickened, stirring occasionally, 5–10 minutes. Mix in the peas and non-dairy milk.

4. Pour the veggie mixture into an extra-deep pie plate or other oven-safe dish. Roll out the pie crust and lay it over the veggie mixture, cutting some slits for steam to escape during cooking. Place the pot pie on a baking sheet to catch any drips.

5. Bake for 25–35 minutes, until the pie crust is lightly golden and the filling is bubbling.

BBQ CAULIFLOWER STEAKS

If you're a BBQ lover, you'll love these cauliflower steaks. They're breaded in a seasoned batter, baked, and then slathered in BBQ-sauce goodness. I love cutting the cauliflower into thick, steak-like slices, but if you prefer, you could also make these into BBQ bites by cutting the cauliflower into florets. Either way, you won't have any problem cleaning your plate.

Prep time: 10 mins (+ 5 mins for the BBQ sauce) • Cook time: 45 mins
Makes: 4-6 cauliflower steaks

1 cauliflower

1 cup non-dairy milk

¾ cup flour (all-purpose, whole wheat, or gluten-free blend)

⅓ cup cornmeal

1 Tbsp maple syrup or agave

1 Tbsp dried basil

2 tsp onion powder

2 tsp garlic powder

2 tsp smoked paprika

½ tsp salt

⅓ cup My Favorite BBQ Sauce (page 209) or store-bought

Cilantro or parsley, chopped, for garnish

1. Preheat your oven to 450°F. Line a baking sheet with parchment paper.

2. Cut the cauliflower into 1-inch-thick slices. You should get about 4–6. Any florets that fall off can be tossed in the batter and cooked along with the steaks.

3. In a large, flat casserole dish, whisk together the non-dairy milk, flour, cornmeal, maple syrup, basil, onion powder, garlic powder, paprika, and salt to make a thick batter.

4. Dip the cauliflower steaks in the mixture, coating both sides. Lay the slices on the prepared baking sheet.

5. Bake for 25–30 minutes, until the cauliflower is fork tender and the batter is golden. Remove the pan from the oven and brush the BBQ sauce over the steaks, then pop back in the oven for another 10–15 minutes. The BBQ sauce will be sticky and will be just beginning to blacken in some areas. Garnish and serve.

• • • • • • • • • • • • •   Cool Tip   • • • • • • • • • • • • •

Leave the green leaves and stem on the cauliflower while slicing it. It helps hold them together better. You can pick off the leaves after it's sliced.

BETTER THAN TAKE-OUT VEGGIE PAD THAI

There are three deadly sins of take-out veggie pad thai:

1. Ketchup sauce. So not yummy.
2. The noodles are in one big, unslurpable clump.
3. A tiny smattering of vegetables.

My pad thai is just like take-out, except way, way better. No ketchup sauce, no clump-o-noodles, and no shortage of vegetables. Make this, and take-out will be a thing of the past!

Prep time: 5 mins • Cook time: 15 mins • Serves: 4

FOR THE SAUCE

2 cloves garlic, minced

¼ cup soy sauce (gluten-free, if preferred)

1 Tbsp lime juice (1 lime)

2 Tbsp brown sugar, packed

2 Tbsp rice vinegar

¼ tsp crushed red pepper flakes

FOR THE NOODLES

8 oz wide rice noodles (gluten-free, if preferred)

1 Tbsp light oil, like peanut

2 medium carrots, peeled and thinly sliced

1 red bell pepper, sliced

1 yellow onion, sliced

¼ block (3.5 oz) silken or soft tofu

½ cup chopped basil leaves

2 cups mung bean sprouts

½ cup chopped cilantro leaves

¼ cup peanuts, chopped (salted, roasted, raw, whatever you like!)

3 green onions, chopped

1. For the sauce, mix together all the sauce ingredients in a medium bowl. Set aside.

2. Cook the rice noodles according to the package directions. Rinse well under cold water. This is the secret to stopping them from sticking together.

3. Heat the oil in your largest frying pan. Add the carrots, bell pepper, and onion. Cook, stirring constantly, until the veggies have softened and are just beginning to brown, about 5 minutes.

4. Add the tofu. Use a spoon to break it up and scramble it. Now add the cooked noodles, basil, bean sprouts, and the sauce and toss well to combine and heat through. Garnish with cilantro, peanuts, and green onions before serving. Enjoy!

CARAMELIZED ONION PIZZA TO DIE FOR

There is vegan pizza, and then there is THIS vegan pizza. This is, and always will be, the MOST satisfying, movie-night, completely awesome pizza that ever existed in the world of vegan pizza! *(Power stance, fist on hip, thrust pizza cutter to the sky, cue thunder and lightning!)*

Prep time: 5 mins (+ 1 hour 15 mins for the pizza dough)
Cook time: 45-55 mins (+ 35 mins for the tomato sauce + 7 mins for the mozzarella) • Makes: 1 large pizza

1 Tbsp olive oil

1 sweet onion, thinly sliced

1 tsp white sugar

½ tsp salt

1 recipe Go-To Pizza Dough (page 211) or store-bought (gluten-free, if preferred)

½ cup My Family Favorite Tomato Sauce (page 156) or store-bought

½ recipe Life-Changing Mozzarella (page 200) (made with additional water)

1. Preheat your oven to 425°F. Lightly grease a pizza pan or stone.

2. In a large frying pan, heat the oil over low heat. Add the onion, sugar, and salt. Cover and cook for 15 minutes, stirring and adjusting the heat as needed to avoid burning.

3. Remove the lid and continue cooking for 10–15 minutes more, stirring often, until the onions are golden and smell delicious.

4. On a well-floured surface, stretch out the dough to fit your pan. Spread the tomato sauce over the pizza, followed by the mozzarella, and then the onion. Use a fork to help spread the onion around. Bake for 20–25 minutes, until the crust is golden and the cheese is just beginning to brown.

CREAMY ROSÉ LINGUINI

Just tossing around the word "rosé" makes this dish sound all sorts of fancy, and no one will have any idea how easy it is to make. This is the perfect dish for a small dinner party or a date night. I recommend preparing the tomato sauce ahead of time, then pouring yourself a nice glass of wine, and casually stirring in the cashew cream just as your guests arrives. Well, aren't *you* all calm and classy in the kitchen!

Prep time: 5 mins (+ 5 mins for the heavy cream) • Cook time: 35 mins • Serves 4

1 Tbsp olive oil

½ yellow onion, chopped

2 cloves garlic, minced

1 can (28 oz) crushed tomatoes

1 tsp white sugar

¼ tsp salt

¼ tsp black pepper

1 cup Heavenly Heavy Cream (page 206)

1 lb linguini (gluten-free, if preferred)

Handful of basil leaves, plus more for garnish

1. Heat the olive oil in a large frying pan or saucepan over medium heat. Sauté the onion and garlic until the onion softens and begins to brown, about 5 minutes. Stir in the crushed tomatoes (be careful, as the mixture may splatter), along with the sugar, salt, and pepper. Bring the sauce to a simmer and cook for about 15 minutes, stirring every now and then, until the sauce has darkened and cooked down a bit. Stir in the Heavenly Heavy Cream and heat through.

2. In the meantime, cook the linguini according to the package directions.

3. Drain the linguini, then add it to the sauce with the basil. Toss well to combine. Garnish with the remaining basil leaves and serve right away. This dish is best served fresh, but if you have extras, store leftover sauce in an airtight container in the fridge and toss with hot, freshly cooked pasta when you're ready to serve.

•••••• Amper-Uppers ••••••

Stir in ¼ cup vodka to the tomato sauce 10 minutes before adding the Heavenly Heavy Cream to make a vodka rosé sauce!

MEXICAN SWEET POTATO & BLACK BEAN BURRITO

This recipe was inspired by a trip to Mexico. I found a little resto that had some vegan options on the menu, including a giant sweet potato burrito that was calling my name. Wow, was putting sweet potato in a burrito a good idea! It adds such an original flavor, color, and texture—and it takes a burrito from fine to fabulous with one sweep of healthful deliciousness.

Prep time: 10 mins • Cook time: 20 mins • Serves: 4-6

FOR THE SWEET POTATOES AND BLACK BEANS

1 Tbsp oil (olive, canola, coconut all work well)

1 yellow onion, chopped

3 cloves garlic, minced

1 sweet potato, peeled and chopped into ½-inch cubes

½ cup vegetable broth

1 can (19 oz) black beans, drained and rinsed (about 2 cups)

1 tsp chili powder

1 tsp smoked paprika

½ tsp salt

¼ tsp black pepper

FOR THE AVOCADO CILANTRO SAUCE

1 avocado

1 cup cilantro, leaves only (about 1 cup)

½ cup water

1 Tbsp fresh lime juice

1 Tbsp maple syrup or agave

¼ tsp salt

FOR THE BURRITOS

4–6 large tortillas (gluten-free, if preferred)

2 cups shredded lettuce

1. For the sweet potatoes and black beans, place the oil in a large frying pan over medium-high heat. Add the onion, garlic, and sweet potato and sauté for about 5 minutes, until everything just begins to brown. Pour in the vegetable broth, then cover and cook for an additional 6–10 minutes, until the sweet potatoes are cooked through.

2. Add the black beans and spices, and stir well to combine. Cook for another 5 minutes to heat through.

3. For the avocado cilantro sauce, blend all the sauce ingredients in a food processor or blender until mostly smooth.

4. To assemble the burritos, place a large spoonful of bean mixture in the center of a tortilla, then top with lettuce and a big spoonful of avocado cilantro sauce. Fold both the top and bottom of the tortilla in, then roll it up from the sides so the filling is completely enclosed. Heat a dry frying pan over medium-high heat. Once hot, place the burrito, seam side down, in the frying pan. Let toast for a few minutes until golden and the burrito is sealed closed. Flip and toast the other side until golden. Repeat for the other burritos. Serve hot.

LASAGNA FIT FOR A KING (OR A QUEEN)

It's pretty crazy to think that a dish traditionally made from mostly cheese and meat can be veganized, but not only can it be veganized, it will totally rock your taste buds. Layers of creamy mushrooms and spinach, ricotta, and lasagna noodles (and not to mention that vegan mozzarella topping!) make this a great dish to feed a crowd. It can be made ahead of time, and when you serve it with All Hail Caesar Salad (page 77), you've got one fine meal.

Prep time: 10 mins (+ 12 mins for the cheeses + 10-15 mins to rest)
Cook time: 55-65 mins (+ 35 mins for the tomato sauce) • Serves: 6-8

FOR THE MUSHROOMS AND SPINACH

1 Tbsp oil (olive, canola, vegetable all work well)

1 yellow onion, chopped

4 cloves garlic, minced

16 oz mushrooms, sliced

7 cups fresh baby spinach (if using frozen spinach, see cool tip)

1 bunch fresh basil, roughly chopped (set aside some for garnish)

1 recipe Ricotta I Like a Lot-a (page 205)

½ tsp salt

¼ tsp black pepper

TO ASSEMBLE

3 cups My Family Favorite Tomato Sauce (page 156) or store-bought

9–12 lasagna noodles (gluten-free, if preferred), cooked according to package directions

1 recipe Life-Changing Mozzarella (page 200) (made with additional water)

1. Preheat your oven to 375°F.

2. For the mushrooms and spinach, heat the oil in your largest frying pan over medium-high heat. Add the onion, garlic, and mushrooms and sauté for about 5 minutes, until everything has softened. Add the spinach and basil, and cover the pan. Cook for about another 5 minutes, until the spinach is wilted. Remove from the heat, then stir in the ricotta, salt, and pepper.

3. To assemble the lasagna, spread one-quarter of the tomato sauce over the bottom of a 9- x 13-inch baking dish. Add a layer of lasagna noodles, then top with half the mushroom-spinach mixture, and one-third of the remaining tomato sauce, and then another layer of lasagna noodles. Repeat, then top the last layer of lasagna noodles with the remaining tomato sauce and then all of the mozzarella.

4. Cover the lasagna with foil and bake for 20 minutes. Remove the foil and then bake for another 15–20 minutes, until the top begins to brown. Let rest for 10–15 minutes, then garnish with remaining basil before serving.

• • • • • • • • • • • • Cool Tip • • • • • • • • • • • •

If you're using frozen spinach, skip sautéing it, and instead thaw it and squeeze out any excess water before adding it along with the mushrooms and ricotta.

VERY YUMMY HEART OF PALM CAKES

If you're a fish cake kinda person, you'll love these heart of palm cakes. If you aren't a fish cake kinda person, you'll love these heart of palm cakes. These are crispy on the outside, tender in the middle, flavor-packed, and tangy. Ooh là là.

 GLUTEN-FREE

Prep time: 10 mins (+ 5 mins for the mayonnaise) • Cook time: 24 mins
Makes: About 6 patties

FOR THE HEART OF PALM CAKES

2 cans (each 14 oz) hearts of palm, drained and chopped

1 yellow onion, chopped

½ cup flour (all-purpose, whole wheat, gluten-free blend)

2 Tbsp brown sugar, packed

1 tsp dried mustard

½ tsp salt

½ tsp black pepper

¼ tsp smoked paprika

¼ tsp garlic powder

FOR THE TARTAR SAUCE

½ cup Mayonnaise for Days (page 208) or store-bought vegan mayo

2 Tbsp sweet pickle relish

½ tsp dried dill

1. For the heart of palm cakes, place all the ingredients in a large bowl. Use a potato masher to break apart the hearts of palm, and mix everything together until the mixture holds together.

2. Pour enough oil (use a light one, like canola) to cover the bottom of a large frying pan, and put the pan over medium-high heat. When the oil is hot, form a patty with the mixture and drop it directly into the oil, filling the pan with three at a time (or as many as your pan can fit). Fry the patties for 3–6 minutes, until golden on the bottom. Gently flip and repeat on the other side. Repeat with the remaining patties.

3. Make the tartar sauce by mixing everything together in a small bowl. Serve alongside the hot patties. Store leftover patties and tartar sauce in the fridge in airtight containers.

PUMPED-UP PUMPKIN PENNE

Pumpkin is one of those amazingly tasty vegetables that can transition effortlessly from sweet to savory, breakfast all the way to dessert, and from my plate to my belly. Thank you, pumpkin, for being so awesome. Want to know what else is awesome? That this pasta comes together in just 15 minutes and is jam-packed with creamy, pumpkin flavor. It's perfect for a lazy weeknight dinner.

Prep time: 5 mins (+ 5 mins for the heavy cream) • Cook time: 10-15 mins
Serves: 4-6

1 lb penne or other short pasta (gluten-free, if preferred)

1 Tbsp vegan butter

½ yellow onion, chopped

3 cloves garlic, minced

1 can (14 oz) pumpkin purée (not pumpkin pie filling)

1 ½ cups vegetable broth

½ cup Heavenly Heavy Cream (page 206) or full-fat coconut milk

¾ tsp salt

½ tsp black pepper

¼ tsp ground nutmeg

Small handful of fresh sage, chopped

1. Cook the pasta according to the package directions and drain.

2. Meanwhile, in a large saucepan, melt the butter over medium-high heat. Add the onion and garlic and sauté until the onion has softened and is beginning to brown.

3. Stir in all the remaining ingredients and bring to a simmer. Add the pasta to the sauce. Toss well to coat, and serve.

• • • • • • • • • • • • • • Amper-Uppers • • • • • • • • • • • • • •

Remove about 10 fresh sage leaves from their stems and fry them for a minute or two in vegan butter for crispy, buttery leaves. Drain them on a paper towel, and use them to garnish your pasta.

OOH LA LA PUFF PASTRY-WRAPPED LENTIL LOAF

Ok, I admit it, this isn't the most "fuss-free" recipe, but sometimes you want a little bit of fuss, like when you're looking for the most glorious centerpiece for your holiday feast. Well, you've found it in this recipe! This lentil loaf is not only delicious but also completely gorgeous thanks, to the puff pastry. Don't forget to pass the Easiest Gravy in the World (page 209)!

Prep time: 30 mins • Cook time: 1 hour 15 mins–1 hour 25 mins • Makes: 2 (4- x 9-inch) loaves (each serves 5-7)

3 Tbsp ground chia or flax seeds

⅓ cup warm water

1 Tbsp olive oil

4 cloves garlic, minced

2 medium carrots, peeled and chopped

2 stalks celery, chopped

1 yellow onion, chopped

8 oz button mushrooms, sliced (about 1 ½ cups)

1 tsp dried thyme leaves

½ tsp salt

¼ tsp black pepper

¼ tsp cayenne pepper

1 cup uncooked green or brown lentils or 1 can (28 oz) (see Cool Tip)

2 ½ cups vegetable broth (or 1 vegetable bouillon cube, see cool tip)

1 cup toasted walnuts

¾ cup rolled oats

½ cup flour (all-purpose, whole wheat, gluten-free blend)

2 sheets of vegan puff pastry, thawed

3 Tbsp non-dairy milk, like soy or almond

1 recipe Easiest Gravy in the World (page 209), My Favorite BBQ Sauce (page 209), or store-bought vegan BBQ sauce, for serving

1. Preheat your oven to 400°F.

2. In a small bowl, mix the chia into the warm water and set aside.

3. Heat the olive oil in a frying pan over medium-high heat, then sauté the garlic, carrots, celery and onion, until they begin to soften up, about 5 minutes. Add the mushrooms, thyme, salt, pepper, and cayenne and sauté for another 5 minutes, until the mushrooms have shrunk and become juicy. Dump all the veggies into a large bowl and set aside. Return the pan to the heat.

RECIPE CONTINUES

Roll out the puff pastry.

Pat the lentil mixture into a firm loaf.

Cut 1-inch strips down the length of the pastry, then crisscross the strips over the loaf.

Decorate with remaining pieces of puff pastry, brush with non-dairy milk, and bake until golden perfection!

4. Add the lentils to the pan (don't worry about any leftover veggie bits, they'll just add even more flavor). Pour in the vegetable broth, cover, bring to a simmer, and cook, leaving the lid closed and not stirring for 25–30 minutes, until the liquid is absorbed and the lentils are soft and a bit mushy.

4. Add the lentils to the pan (don't worry about any leftover veggie bits, they'll just add even more flavor). Pour in the vegetable broth, cover, bring to a simmer, and cook, leaving the lid closed and not stirring for 25–30 minutes, until the liquid is absorbed and the lentils are soft and a bit mushy.

5. Use a potato masher to smash the lentils until about two-thirds of them are mush. This lentil mush makes everything hold together nicely. Yum, mushy! Add the lentils to the veggies and then add the chia, walnuts, oats, and flour. Mix well.

6. On a lightly floured surface, roll out one of the puff pastry sheets into a rectangle that is about 10 x 14 inches. Place it on top of a sheet of parchment paper.

7. Now, braid wrap your lentil loaf. Use the back of a knife to lightly score a guide dividing the pastry into three even sections lengthwise. Cut strips down each side about 1 inch wide. Cut off the top and bottom corners, so that you have two end flaps. Place half of the lentil mixture down the center of the dough and, using your hands, pat it into a firm loaf shape. Fold up the top flap over the end, then take the top left strip and fold it over the loaf. Take the top right strip, and fold that over, making an *x*. Do this all the way down, alternating strips. Try to keep the strips close together, leaving only small gaps between them. Once you get near the bottom, fold the bottom flap up, then finish braiding the last strips by tucking the ends in anywhere they look good. You can use the remaining pieces of pastry to cut little leaf shapes, or any shape you like, and tuck them into the weave. Repeat with the remaining pastry and lentil mixture so you have two loaves.

8. Brush the tops with non-dairy milk and lift the parchment paper and loaf onto a baking sheet. Bake for 40–45 minutes, checking every now and then until it's all golden brown and gorgeous. Serve with onion gravy or your favorite BBQ sauce heated up.

• • • • • • • • • Cool Tip • • • • • • • • •

This lentil loaf can also be made without the puff pastry for an easier weeknight meal. Instead of wrapping the filling in puff pastry, press it into a 4- x 8-inch loaf pan lined with parchment paper, brush the top with My Favorite BBQ Sauce (page 209) to keep it moist, then bake 400°F for 40–45 minutes.

The lentil mixture can be prepared ahead of time, popped into an airtight container and stored in the fridge or freezer. Then just thaw, wrap in the puff pastry and bake according to the directions.

For faster prep, skip cooking the lentils from scratch in step 4 (so, you won't need the broth for this option). Instead, drain and rinse a 28 oz can of lentils, add them to the bowl of veggies as in step 5, then crumble over a vegetable bouillon cube, and follow the remaining directions from step 5 onward.

THE VEGAN MAC & CHEESE THAT ALL CHEESE LOVERS ADORE

This recipe is serious stuff, my friends. Mac and cheese isn't a joke, and this recipe proves it. Don't be fooled by how simple it is to make. When I served it to my omnivore friends and family, not only was everyone blown away by how delicious it was and wowed that it was indeed vegan, but they literally couldn't stop eating it until it was gone. Never once have I had any leftovers.

Cook time: 15 mins (+ 7 mins for the nacho cheese) • Serves: 4

2 ½ cups macaroni or other short pasta (gluten-free, if preferred)

1 recipe Nacho Cheese Love (page 201)

¼–½ cup non-dairy milk, divided

¾ tsp salt, plus more to taste

1. Cook the pasta according to the package directions until al dente.

2. Drain the pasta, return it to the saucepan, and add the Nacho Cheese Love, ¼ cup of the non-dairy milk, and salt. Mix well so that the pasta melts the cheese and it mixes in. Add more non-dairy milk and salt to taste.

FAB VEGGIE FRIED RICE

This is a great recipe for using up leftover rice, but it's so tasty that it's totally worth cooking rice just to make this. The key here is that the rice has to be cold. If it's warm, it will stick together in rice blobs. Cold rice grains won't stick together when they're reheated, so it can be properly mixed and fried. Then, once you've got the rice nailed, it's all about the fresh veggies, the zing of garlic and ginger, and my not-so-secret favorite addition, salted roasted cashews or peanuts.

30 minutes or less

GLUTEN-FREE

Prep time: 10 mins • Cook time: 10 mins (+ 20-40 mins for the rice) • Serves: 4

1 Tbsp light oil (such as canola or peanut oil)

2 medium carrots, peeled and chopped

1 yellow onion, chopped

1 red bell pepper, chopped

1-inch piece fresh ginger, minced

3 cloves garlic, minced

4 cups cold cooked white or brown rice (leftover works great!)

3 green onions, sliced

1 cup fresh or frozen peas

½ cup salted roasted cashews or peanuts

¼ cup gluten-free soy sauce

2 tsp sesame oil

1. In a large nonstick pan, heat the oil over medium-high heat. Add the carrots, onion, bell pepper, ginger, and garlic. Sauté until the veggies are softened and beginning to brown, about 5 minutes.

2. Crank the heat to high, and add the rice, along with all of the remaining ingredients. Stir-fry until everything is heated through, about 5 more minutes.

SMOKY SUN-DRIED TOMATO PIZZA

Vegan pepperoni is usually available in your average grocery store, but why bother with expensive processed stuff when you can get an even better flavor from a whole food? These marinated sun-dried tomatoes are smoky sweet and delightfully chewy, making them a perfect pizza topping!

 GLUTEN-FREE

Prep time: 10 mins–1 hour to marinate (+ 1 hour 15 mins for pizza dough + 7 mins for the cheese) • Cook time: 25 mins (+ 35 mins for the tomato sauce) • Makes: 1 large pizza

FOR THE SMOKY SUN-DRIED TOMATOES

2 tsp soy sauce (gluten-free, if preferred)

1 tsp olive oil

½ tsp dried oregano

½ tsp maple syrup

¼ tsp liquid smoke

¼ tsp black pepper

½ cup sun-dried tomatoes, chopped

FOR THE PIZZA

1 recipe Go-To Pizza Dough (page 211) or store-bought (gluten-free, if preferred)

½ cup My Family Favorite Tomato Sauce (page 156) or store-bought

1 recipe Life-Changing Mozzarella (page 200)

¼ cup fresh basil, chopped (optional)

½ tsp crushed red pepper flakes (optional)

1. Preheat your oven to 425°F. Lightly grease a pizza pan or round baking pan.

2. For the smoky sun-dried tomatoes, in a medium bowl, mix together the soy sauce, olive oil, oregano, maple syrup, liquid smoke, and pepper. Add the sun-dried tomatoes and mix well to coat thoroughly in the marinade. Let marinate at room temperature for 10 minutes to 1 hour.

3. For the pizza, stretch out the dough on a well-floured surface to fit your pan. Spread the tomato sauce over the dough, then spread the mozzarella over top. Bake for 15 minutes, then pull out of the oven and quickly scatter the sun-dried tomatoes over the mozzarella. Bake the pizza for another 5–10 minutes, until the crust is golden brown. Keep a close eye on the sun-dried tomatoes so they don't burn. Sprinkle with basil and red pepper flakes (if using), and serve hot.

• • • • • • • • • • • • • • •   Cool Tip   • • • • • • • • • • • • • • •

If you are using sun-dried tomatoes that come in oil, drain off as much oil as possible and omit the olive oil in the marinade.

MY FAMILY FAVORITE TOMATO SAUCE

A gorgeous homemade tomato sauce always reminds me of home. At least once a week (likely more), my mom, my dad, or I would be in the kitchen preparing a fresh sauce. We all have our own personal tweaks, but the end result is always eagerly devoured by the whole family. While store-bought tomato sauces can be fine for using in recipes such as lasagna and on pizza, I very much prefer this homemade version when the sauce is the focus of the dish.

Prep time: 5 mins • Cook time: 35 mins • Serves: 4

1 Tbsp olive oil

½ yellow onion, chopped

3 cloves garlic, minced

2 cans (each 28 oz) whole tomatoes

1 Tbsp white sugar

1 tsp dried basil

1 tsp dried oregano

½ tsp salt

¼ tsp black pepper

1. Warm the olive oil in a large frying pan over medium-high heat. Add the onion and garlic and sauté until the onion softens and begins to brown, about 5 minutes.

2. Now add the whole tomatoes, liquid and all, the sugar, basil, oregano, salt, and pepper.

3. For a chunkier sauce (my fave), use a potato masher to mash up all of the tomatoes. For a smoother sauce, use an immersion blender to blend all the tomatoes.

4. Bring to a simmer and cook for 20–30 minutes, stirring every now and then, until the sauce has darkened in color and everything comes together. If the sauce cooks down too much, just splash in a bit of water until the desired consistency is reached.

• • • • • • • • • • • • • • • • Cool Tip • • • • • • • • • • • • • • •

I like using whole canned tomatoes, because I find the flavor is much better and you can control the texture of the sauce to your preference.

SWEET
Tooth

I have a sweet spot in my heart for baking (clever pun, I know). You see, my mom was one of those good, healthy moms, so we rarely had candies or anything sugary in the house. I learned at a pretty young age that if I wanted a sweet treat, the best route was to make it myself. Chocolate chip cookies were my go-to, but I was also brave enough to tackle more complicated desserts, like checkerboard cookies, multi-layer cakes, homemade ice creams, and anything I found in cooking magazines.

So, the recipes in this chapter are not only near and dear to my childhood heart, but they were some of the most rewarding ones to create. Baking without eggs and dairy? No problemo.

GLORIOUSLY CHEWY CHOCOLATE CHIP COOKIES

In my opinion, there is no better cookie than a good old-fashioned chocolate chip cookie, and this version is the ULTIMATE in chocolate chip cookies. Even two or three days after baking, they'll still be soft and chewy (not that they'll last that long).

Prep time: 10 mins • Cook time: 14-18 mins • Makes: 14-16 large cookies

DRY INGREDIENTS

1 ¾ cups all-purpose flour

¾ tsp baking soda

¼ tsp salt

WET INGREDIENTS

½ cup white sugar

½ cup brown sugar, packed

2 tsp vanilla extract

¾ cup vegan butter

¾ cup vegan chocolate chips

1. Preheat your oven to 350°F. Lightly grease a baking sheet.

2. Mix the dry ingredients together in a large bowl.

3. In a medium bowl, beat all the wet ingredients together except for the chocolate chips until creamy. Add the wet ingredients to the dry ingredients and mix until just combined. I find different vegan butter brands have different moisture contents, so if you find the dough is a little dry, add up to 1 Tbsp water until the dough holds together. Now mix in the chocolate chips.

4. Using 2 tablespoons of dough per cookie, roll the dough into balls and place them about 3 inches apart on the baking sheet. Bake for 14–18 minutes, until golden. The cookies wil have spread, but will look almost raw. They should be golden on the underside. I promise they'll be perfectly chewy once they've cooled on the pan.

•••••••••••••••• Cool Tip ••••••••••••••••

Here's a sneaky trick food photographers and bakeries use to make the most perfect-looking chocolate chip cookies: Set aside about ¼ cup of the chocolate chips. Instead of stirring them into the batter with the rest of the chocolate chips, roll your cookie balls, and press several chocolate chips on top of each dough ball. They'll look perfect once baked!

24 KARAT CARROT CAKE

This sweet, moist, spiced to perfection, jam-packed with carrot-y goodness cake tastes like it walked straight out of a fancy-schmancy bakery and right into your kitchen. Except, not walked, because that would be creepy . . . and, ahem, not vegan.

Prep time: 15 mins (+ 5 mins for the frosting) • Cook time: 18-38 mins
Makes: 1 (two-layer 9-inch) cake or 24 cupcakes

DRY INGREDIENTS

2 ½ cups all-purpose flour

1 Tbsp ground cinnamon

2 tsp baking soda

½ tsp salt

¼ tsp ground nutmeg

1 cup chopped pecans or walnuts (optional)

WET INGREDIENTS

3 cups grated carrots (about 3 medium carrots)

1 ⅓ cups non-dairy milk (such as soy or almond)

¾ cup white sugar

¾ cup brown sugar, packed

⅔ cup light oil (such as canola or vegetable)

¼ cup fresh lemon juice (1–2 lemons)

1 Tbsp vanilla extract

You Won't Believe It's Cream Cheese Frosting (page 170)

Handful of chopped walnuts (optional)

1. Preheat your oven to 350°F. Lightly grease two round 9-inch cake pans or line the wells of a cupcake pan with 24 paper liners.

2. In a large bowl, whisk together all the dry ingredients except the nuts.

3. In a medium bowl, mix together the wet ingredients. Add the wet ingredients to the dry and mix until the batter just comes together. Do not overmix. Evenly divide the batter among the cake pans or cupcake liners.

4. For the 9-inch cakes, bake for 32–38 minutes, until golden on top and a toothpick inserted into the center comes out clean. Allow to cool completely in the pan before removing.

5. For the cupcakes, bake for 18–20 minutes, until the tops are slightly golden and a toothpick inserted into the center comes out clean. Let cool completely before frosting. Decorate the top with walnuts, if using, and serve!

THE BEST VANILLA CAKE

So, here it is. This is my recipe for the most perfect, bestest in the westest (and eastest) vegan vanilla cake . . . Actually, strike that. This is my idea of the most perfect vanilla cake. Period. Vegan or not, this is a damn good cake. When I served this to a friend, she said it was so good it made her want to laugh!

Less than **10** ingredients

Prep time: 15 mins • Cook time: 18–40 mins
Makes: 1 (two-layer 9-inch) cake or 24 cupcakes

DRY INGREDIENTS

2 ½ cups all-purpose flour

1 ½ cups white sugar

2 tsp baking soda

1 tsp salt

WET INGREDIENTS

1 ⅓ cups non-dairy milk (such as soy or almond)

⅔ cup light oil (such as canola or vegetable)

¼ cup fresh lemon juice (1–2 lemons) or apple cider vinegar

1 Tbsp vanilla extract

1. Preheat your oven to 350°F. Lightly grease two 9-inch round cake pans or line the wells of a cupcake pan with 24 paper liners.

2. In a large bowl, whisk together the dry ingredients.

3. In a medium bowl, mix together the wet ingredients. Add the wet ingredients to the dry ingredients. Mix until the batter just comes together. Do not overmix, or your cupcakes will be sad cakes. Evenly divide the batter among the cake pans or cupcake liners.

4. For the 9-inch cakes, bake for 22–28 minutes, until golden on top and a toothpick inserted in the center comes out clean. Let cool completely before removing from the pan.

5. For the cupcakes, bake for 18–20 minutes, until the tops are slightly golden and a toothpick inserted into the center comes out clean. Let cool completely and decorate with your favorite frosting, if desired (see pages 168–171 for some inspiration).

SINFULLY RICH CHOCOLATE CAKE

It is time, my friends, for the most ridiculously awesome, ultimate vegan chocolate cake. Applause, please. Thank you. (I'm subtle, I know.) This cake is rich, moist, fudge-y, and super . . . what's the word? . . . oh, chocolatey. That's really the best word to describe it. This is no light and fluffy nonsense of a chocolate cake. This cake is really rich, and I promise you that no one will notice it's vegan. I wouldn't be surprised if non-vegans asked for the recipe, and then you can be all cool with your sweet self, and pass it along, and wink when you tell them it's vegan.

Prep time: 15 mins • Cook time: 18-40 mins • Makes: 1 (two-layer 9-inch) cake or 24 cupcakes

DRY INGREDIENTS

2 ½ cups all-purpose flour

2 ½ cups white sugar

1 cup cocoa powder

1 tsp salt

1 tsp baking powder

½ tsp baking soda

WET INGREDIENTS

2 ⅔ cups non-dairy milk (such as soy or almond)

⅔ cup light oil (such as canola or vegetable)

2 Tbsp apple cider vinegar

1 Tbsp vanilla extract

1. Preheat your oven to 350°F. Lightly grease two 9-inch round cake pans or line the wells of a cupcake pan with 24 paper liners.

2. In a large bowl, whisk together the dry ingredients.

3. In a medium bowl, mix together the wet ingredients. Add the wet ingredients to the dry ingredients. Mix until the batter just comes together. Do not overmix. Evenly divide the batter among the cake pans or cupcake liners.

4. For the 9-inch cakes, bake for 35–40 minutes, until golden on top and a toothpick inserted into the center comes out clean. Cool completely before removing from the pan.

5. For the cupcakes, bake for 20–25 minutes, until the tops are slightly golden. Let cool completely before decorating with your favorite frosting, if you want. I prefer the Fluffy Chocolate Frosting on page 171.

WHIPPED VANILLA FROSTING

So fluffy, so frosting-y. Cake just isn't cake without the frosting, and you need this so fluffy, so frosting-y frosting in your life. Just make sure you let your cake completely cool before slapping on this whipped goodness.

Prep time: 5 mins • Makes: Enough frosting for 1 two-layer (9-inch) cake or 24 cupcakes, about 3 cups

½ cup vegetable shortening (I prefer non-hydrogenated)

½ cup vegan butter

3 cups icing sugar

1 tsp vanilla extract

1–4 Tbsp non-dairy milk (such as soy or almond) (if needed)

1. Use a mixer (hand-held or stand) to cream the shortening and vegan butter, then mix in the icing sugar and vanilla until whipped and creamy. If the frosting is a bit too stiff, add the non-dairy milk, 1 Tbsp at a time, until the desired consistency is reached. Store in an airtight container in the fridge or freezer (thaw before using).

•••••••• Cool Tip ••••••••

Add a few drops of vegan food coloring to jazz up your frosting.

•••••••••••••••••• Vegan Tidbit ••••••••••••••••••

I use a combo of vegetable shortening and vegan butter in this recipe. I find that provides the best stability. If you prefer, you can use all vegan butter, but try to use little to no non-dairy milk if you do that, and keep the cake in a cool place so the frosting doesn't melt.

YOU WON'T BELIEVE IT'S CREAM CHEESE FROSTING

Before veganism, if I had looked at this recipe, I would have thought, "Apple cider vinegar in frosting!? Ew." Good thing I've learned since then, because I swear that for whatever magical reason, it makes this frosting taste just like traditional cream cheese frosting. You won't believe it until you try it!

Prep time: 5 mins • **Makes:** Enough frosting for 1 (two-layer 9-inch) cake or 24 cupcakes, about 3 cups

½ cup vegetable shortening (I prefer non-hydrogenated)

½ cup vegan butter

3 cups icing sugar

1 Tbsp apple cider vinegar

2 tsp vanilla extract

1 tsp fresh lemon juice

1–2 Tbsp non-dairy milk (such as soy or almond)

1. Use a mixer (hand-held or stand) to cream the shortening and vegan butter, then mix in the icing sugar, apple cider vinegar, vanilla, and lemon juice until whipped and creamy. If the frosting is a bit too stiff, add the non-dairy milk, 1–2 Tbsp at a time, until the desired consistency is reached.

• • • • • • • • • • • • • • • Vegan Tidbit • • • • • • • • • • • • • • • •

As with all my frostings, I use a combo of vegetable shortening and vegan butter for the best texture. If you only have vegan butter, you can use that, but note that the frosting will be softer, so use little to no non-dairy milk, and store the frosted cake in a cool place.

FLUFFY CHOCOLATE FROSTING

Are you an eat-the-frosting-first kinda person? Perfect. This is the recipe for you. Soft, fluffy, choco-latey, lick-the-spoon frosting perfection. You're going to want to shove the cake aside and eat the frosting first!

Prep time: 5 mins • Makes: Enough frosting for 1 (two-layer 9-inch) cake or 24 cupcakes, about 3 ½ cups

½ cup vegetable shortening (I prefer non-hydrogenated)

½ cup vegan butter

1 ¼ cups icing sugar

¼ cup cocoa powder

1 tsp vanilla extract

1–2 Tbsp non-dairy milk (such as soy or almond) (if needed)

1. Use a mixer (hand-held or stand) to cream the shortening and vegan butter, then mix in the icing sugar, cocoa, and vanilla until whipped and creamy. If the frosting is a bit too stiff, add non-dairy milk, 1 Tbsp at a time, until the desired consistency is reached. Store frosting in an airtight container in the fridge or freezer (thaw before using).

•••••••••••••••••••• Vegan Tidbit ••••••••••••••••••••

Mixing vegetable shortening and vegan butter together makes for the best stability. If shortening ain't your thang, you can use all vegan butter, but use as little non-dairy milk as needed for a thick frosting, and keep it in a cool place so it doesn't melt.

CRISPY CARAMEL RICE SQUARES

Most marshmallows contain gelatin, which we know isn't vegan-friendly. You can find vegan marshmallows at health food stores, but one day I had a burning desire for crispy rice squares and I had no vegan marshmallows on hand, so I had to get creative. This is the recipe I invented, with ingredients I already had around the house, and I'm so glad that I did! Crispy, caramel squares for the win!

Prep time: 30 mins to chill • Cook time: 12–17 mins • Makes: 1 (9- x 13-inch) pan

1 ¾ cups full-fat coconut milk

¾ cup white sugar

¼ cup agave or maple syrup

2 Tbsp vegan butter

½ tsp vanilla extract

6 cups puffed rice cereal

• • • • • • Amper-Uppers • • • • • •

For salted caramel crispy rice squares, lightly sprinkle ¼ tsp flaked salt across the top before they set.

1. Lightly grease a 9- x 13-inch baking dish.

2. Place the coconut milk, sugar, agave, and vegan butter in a large saucepan and mix to combine. Bring to a boil over medium-high heat and then turn down to simmer. Simmer for 15–20 minutes, stirring often until the mixture is a rich golden caramel color, the bubbling decreases, and the mixture begins to thicken. It will smell like marshmallows!

3. Remove from the heat and whisk in the vanilla. Then add the puffed rice cereal and stir well to combine. Pour into the prepared pan, and spread and pat down with a spatula. Chill, uncovered, in the fridge for 30 minutes or until set. Slice into bars and enjoy. Keep the squares in an airtight container in the fridge for up to a week, and serve cold; they soften as they warm.

BLENDER PUMPKIN PIE

This is one of the best pies I have ever had. No lie. I'm not trying to pat myself on the back, I'm just being honest here. My testing involved feeding it not only to myself (repeatedly . . . for testing purposes, of course), but also to several non-vegan folk. Everyone agreed: Hands down, yum! More. Now. Please? Pretty, pretty please!? This pie will become a staple at your holiday feasts.

 GLUTEN-FREE

Prep time: 5 mins (+ 15 mins for the pie crust + at least 4 hours to chill)
Cook time: 1 hour • Makes: 1 (9-inch) pie (serves 6–8)

1 recipe My Nana's Perfect Pie Crust (page 214) or 1 store-bought vegan pie crust (gluten-free, if preferred)

1 can (14 oz) pumpkin purée (not pumpkin pie filling)

¾ cup full-fat coconut milk

½ cup brown sugar, packed

¼ cup maple syrup

¼ cup cornstarch

2 tsp pumpkin pie spice

1 tsp vanilla extract

½ tsp ground cinnamon

½ tsp salt

1. Preheat your oven to 350°F. Line a 9-inch pie plate with the pastry.

2. Place the pumpkin purée, coconut milk, brown sugar, maple syrup, cornstarch, pumpkin pie spice, vanilla, cinnamon, and salt in a blender or a large bowl. Mix well to combine. Pour this pumpkin mixture into the uncooked pie crust, and spread it out evenly with a spatula.

3. Bake for 1 hour. When you remove it from the oven, the edges might be slightly cracked and the middle will still look very wobbly. Let cool at room temperature, then chill in fridge, uncovered, for a minimum of 4 hours until set, or preferably overnight. Serve with a dollop of Magical Coconut Whipped Cream (page 181) if you desire.

INSTANT VANILLA ICE CREAM

Nice cream is very popular across the Internet. It's simply frozen bananas blended into a creamy soft serve, sometimes with some extras thrown in. But what if you're in the mood for instant ice cream and frozen bananas just aren't going to cut it? Well, welcome, my friends. This way, take a seat, be prepared to fall in love. I have figured out a way to make instant ice cream that is seriously sensational.

Prep time: 5 mins + overnight to freeze • Makes: About 2 cups

1 ¾ cups full-fat coconut milk OR Heavenly Heavy Cream (page 206)

3 Tbsp maple syrup or agave

Seeds scraped from ½ vanilla bean, or 1 ½ tsp vanilla extract

1 Tbsp–¼ cup non-dairy milk (such as soy or almond) (if needed)

1. Pour the coconut milk into ice cube trays. Freeze overnight until solid.

2. Pop out the frozen cubes into a food processor or high-speed blender and add the maple syrup and vanilla seeds. Blend until smooth and creamy, stopping to scrape down the sides as needed. If your mixture is too thick, splash in a bit of non-dairy milk, 1 Tbsp at a time, to help thin.

3. This ice cream will have a soft serve texture. For a firmer ice cream, just pop it in the freezer, in a loaf pan or another freezer-friendly container, for 30 minutes to an hour to firm up. Store leftovers in the freezer.

• • • • • • • • • • • • • • • •   Cool Tip   • • • • • • • • • • • • • • • •

If you want to have ice cream at the ready, make a bunch of trays of frozen coconut cubes or Heavenly Heavy Cream cubes, and just toss them in a freezer-friendly bag. Ice cream fix is ready to go!

Chocolate

Add 3 Tbsp cocoa powder and 1 extra Tbsp maple syrup or agave.

Double Chocolate

Add 3 Tbsp cocoa powder, plus an additional 1 Tbsp maple syrup
or agave. Once the ice cream is smooth, add 2 Tbsp vegan
chocolate chips and pulse to incorporate.

Cookies 'n' Cream

Once the ice cream is smooth, add ¼ cup crumbled chocolate creme
cookies and pulse to incorporate.

Cookie Dough

Roll ¼ cup Gloriously Chewy Chocolate Chip Cookies dough
(page 161) into small balls. Once the ice cream is smooth,
add the cookie dough balls and pulse to incorporate.
(You can prepare a full batch of the cookie dough ahead
of time and store the mini balls in the freezer so they're
ready to go for ice cream at any time.)

Chocolate Chip

Once the ice cream is smooth, add 2 Tbsp vegan chocolate chips
and pulse to incorporate.

Mint Chocolate Chip

Add a handful of mint leaves and blend. Once the ice cream is
smooth, add 2 Tbsp vegan chocolate chips and pulse to incorporate.

Chocolate Peanut Butter

Add 3 Tbsp cocoa powder and 1 extra Tbsp maple syrup or agave.
Once the ice cream is smooth, drizzle in 2 Tbsp all-natural
peanut butter and pulse to swirl in.

Coffee

Add 2 tsp instant espresso powder before blending.

Mocha

Add 3 Tbsp cocoa powder, 2 tsp instant espresso powder, and
1 extra Tbsp maple syrup or agave before blending.

INSTANT FRUIT ICE CREAM

To complete the world of fuss-free vegan ice cream, we need a fruit-based ice cream. Strawberry ice cream is a total classic and one of my faves, so we can't forget about it! The amazing thing about this recipe is that it's even more instant than the vanilla ice cream recipe (is more instant a thing?) No need to think ahead and freeze coconut milk; use frozen fruit and you're good to go!

Prep time: 5 mins (+ 5 mins for the heavy cream) • Makes: About 2 cups

3 cups frozen fruit (strawberries, blueberries, cherries, bananas, peaches, mango, etc.)

¼–½ cup Heavenly Heavy Cream (page 206) or full-fat coconut milk

3 Tbsp maple syrup or agave

½ tsp vanilla extract

1. Place the frozen fruit, ¼ cup of the Heavenly Heavy Cream, the maple syrup, and vanilla in a food processor or high-speed blender and process until smooth and creamy, stopping to scrape the sides as needed. Add more cream as needed to reach the desired consistency.

2. This ice cream will have a soft serve texture. For a firmer ice cream, just pop it in the freezer for 30 minutes to 1 hour to set up.

• • • • • • • • • • • • • • • Cool Tip • • • • • • • • • • • • • • •

Use one type of fruit for a simple ice cream, but feel free to experiment with fruit combos. Mixed berry or a tropical combo of bananas and mangoes are both delicious.

MAGICAL COCONUT WHIPPED CREAM

You can have your cream and whip it too! With only two ingredients and some good old-fashioned whipping action, this whipped cream is so ridiculously easy to make. Unlike with traditional whipped cream, you aren't taking a liquid and whipping it into a cream; instead, you're taking chilled solid coconut cream and breaking it down into a whipped cream.

Prep time: 5 mins + overnight to chill the coconut milk beforehand
Makes: About 1¼ cups

1 ¾ cups premium coconut milk or coconut cream (see Tidbit below)

2 Tbsp icing sugar

1. Put the can of coconut milk in the coldest spot of your fridge overnight. (I always keep a couple cans in the back of my fridge for emergencies that require whipped cream.)

2. When you're ready to make the whipped cream, remove the can from the fridge, open, and scoop out all of the hardened coconut cream, leaving any water behind. Add the coconut cream to a bowl along with the icing sugar.

3. Beat until whipped and lovely. If you find it a bit thick, add 1 Tbsp of the coconut water or non-dairy milk at a time to thin as needed.

• • • • • • • • • • • • • • • Vegan Tidbit • • • • • • • • • • • • • • •

The key here is to find the right coconut milk. Many of the cans of coconut milk in stores are actually made from coconut extract, and this won't produce a whipped cream. You want the real stuff! Look for "premium" coconut milk, or "coconut cream." Or if you don't see that, pick up the cans and shake them. The less liquid you hear sloshing around, the better. You might have to test out some brands until you find the ones that work best for whipping. You will know it's a good one when you get a lot of hardened cream once chilled overnight.

FUDGY DOUBLE CHOCOLATE BROWNIES

These brownies are every bit as fudgy and chocolatey as a good brownie should be. The edges are lightly crisp and the center is chewy and full of rich chocolatey goodness. My sneaky-deaky trick to making perfect fudgy brownies is to let them rest overnight. But if you can't wait to dig in, go for it; the brownies will just be soft and crumbly—perfect for crumbling them over top of Instant Vanilla Ice Cream (page 176) for a real treat. If you're having a wicked chocolate craving, these will be your new best friend!

Prep time: 10 mins (+ overnight to cool before cutting) • Cook time: 30-35 mins
Makes: 1 (8- x 8-inch) pan (12 brownies)

1 cup vegan chocolate chips

½ cup vegan butter

1 cup white sugar

½ cup non-dairy milk (such as soy or almond)

1 tsp vanilla extract

½ cup all-purpose flour

¼ cup cocoa powder

1 ½ tsp baking powder

¼ tsp salt

½ cup chopped walnuts (optional)

1. Preheat your oven to 350°F. Grease an 8- x 8-inch baking pan.

2. In a small saucepan, melt together the chocolate chips and butter, making sure to remove the saucepan from the heat just as it's finished melting to ensure you don't burn the chocolate.

3. Pour the melted chocolate into a mixing bowl. Add the sugar, non-dairy milk, and vanilla and mix well. Now add the flour, cocoa, baking powder, and salt and mix until combined. Finally, add the walnuts (if using).

4. Pour the batter into the prepared baking pan and bake for 30–35 minutes, until the brownies are pulling away from the sides of the pan and a toothpick inserted in the center comes out with just a few moist crumbs on it. Let the brownies cool and set overnight. This is the key to perfect gooey brownies.

5. To store, let the brownies cool completely, then cover with foil or plastic wrap and keep at room temperature for the best texture. For longer storage put in an airtight container and store in the fridge.

CRÈME BRÛLÉE (YES, REALLY)

Anything can be veganized. I repeat, ANYTHING CAN BE VEGANIZED! What I love most about this crème brûlée recipe (apart from its incredibly scrumptious taste) is that it's even easier to make than the traditional recipe. You see, in the traditional recipe, the custards are cooked in a *bain-marie*, which is just a bath of hot water. Well, I ain't got time for that. All you have to do in my recipe is simmer the custard until it thickens, pour it into ramekins, and let it set overnight in the fridge. Then, when ready to serve, sprinkle with sugar, whip out the torch, and brûlée (AKA: brown that sugar). Spoon at the ready? Good. Now crack that sugar and dig in deep!

Prep time: overnight to set • Cook time: 5–8 mins • Serves: 4–6

½ cup non-dairy milk (such as soy or almond)

3 Tbsp cornstarch

1 can (14 oz) full-fat coconut milk

½ cup white sugar

1 tsp nutritional yeast

Seeds scraped from 1 vanilla bean or 1 tsp vanilla extract

⅛ tsp black salt or regular salt

Pinch of turmeric for color (optional)

4–6 tsp sugar for topping (1 tsp per crème brûlée)

1. In a small bowl, mix the non-dairy milk with the cornstarch. Set aside.

2. In a medium saucepan, whisk the coconut milk, with the sugar, nutritional yeast, vanilla, salt, and turmeric. Bring to a simmer over medium heat. Once it's simmering, slowly pour in the cornstarch mixture, stirring constantly while it thickens, about 1 minute.

3. Divide the mixture among 4–6 ramekins, teacups, or small bowls. Let cool on the counter for 10 minutes, then cover with plastic wrap, and cool completely in the fridge overnight.

4. When you're ready to serve the brûlée, simply sprinkle about 1 tsp sugar over the top of each custard. Give each dish a little shake to flatten the sugar out, then with a brûlée torch, brown the sugar by moving the torch around, keeping it about 2–3 inches from the sugar, until the surface is all golden and yummy.

SILKY CHOCOLATE FUDGE

Many fudge recipes require candy thermometers, and by now I think you've probably picked up on the fact that I just so don't have the time, or patience, for those kinds of recipes. Oddly enough, I used to as a kid, but now, with my busy schedule, I'm all about the quick and easy, and, well, fuss-free. So, it was my goal to create a silky, rich, melt-in-your-mouth chocolate fudge that is as easy to make as it is tasty. Here you go, my friends. Silky fudge is coming your way!

Prep time: 1–3 hours to set • Cook time: 5 mins
Makes: 1 (8- x 8-inch) pan (about 12 pieces)

1 cup full-fat coconut milk

3 cups vegan chocolate chips

2 cups icing sugar

1 Tbsp instant espresso powder (optional for added kick)

1 cup walnuts or pecans, roughly chopped (optional)

1. Line an 8- x 8-inch pan with enough parchment paper so that the paper hangs over the sides to form handles.

2. Heat the coconut milk in a saucepan over medium heat. When it comes to a boil, lower the heat and whisk in the chocolate chips. As soon as they've melted, remove the mixture from the heat and add the icing sugar and espresso powder (if using). Use an immersion blender to blend until completely smooth. (You can whisk in the sugar by hand, but it may be difficult to get rid of all the lumps.) Stir in the walnuts or pecans (if using).

3. Pour the batter into the prepared pan and spread it out evenly. Place it in the fridge for 3 hours or in the freezer for 1 hour to firm up before slicing.

LEMON MERINGUE PIE
(THAT EVEN FOOLS MY SISTER)

My sister LOVES lemon meringue pie—so much so that she has become quite the connoisseur. When I served her my first attempt at a veganized version, she had some serious critiques. So I went back to the kitchen, and eventually emerged with this recipe, which got rave reviews. My sneaky trick is to use aquafaba (the liquid you find in cans of chickpeas). When whipped, it foams up just the same as egg whites. It's miraculous!

   This pie taste exactly the same as the traditional version, for real, folks. Sister-approved.

Prep time: 20 mins (+ at least 4 hours to chill) • Cook time: 25-30 mins (+ 15 mins for the pie crust) • Makes: 1 (9-inch) pie (serves 6-8)

FOR THE CRUST
1 recipe My Nana's Perfect Pie Crust (page 214) or store-bought pie crust (gluten-free, if preferred)

FOR THE LEMON FILLING
1 ¼ cups white sugar

¼ cup cornstarch

¼ tsp salt

1 cup water

½ cup fresh lemon juice (2–3 lemons)

½ cup of your favorite non-dairy milk

2 Tbsp vegan butter

¼ tsp ground turmeric

½ tsp vanilla extract

FOR THE MERINGUE
¾ cup aquafaba

6 Tbsp white sugar

½ tsp vanilla extract

¼ tsp cream of tartar

1. Line a 9-inch pie dish with the pastry, and bake according to the method on page 214, or according to package directions.

2. For the filling, in a medium saucepan, whisk together the sugar, cornstarch, and salt. Now add the water, lemon juice, non-dairy milk, vegan butter, and turmeric. Put it over medium heat and bring to a simmer. Cook for about 5 minutes, stirring often until it thickens. Remove from the heat and whisk in the vanilla. Pour into the prepared pie crust. Let cool completely in the fridge for about 4 hours or overnight.

3. Preheat your oven to 300°F.

4. When ready to bake, prepare the meringue. Beat the aquafaba together with the sugar, vanilla, and cream of tartar until stiff peaks form. With some mixers this can take as long as 15 minutes, so be patient—it will fluff up eventually. Spread the meringue over the pie and use a spatula to make pretty designs and peaks.

5. Bake for 20–25 minutes, until the meringue is lightly browned on top. Let cool completely before serving.

•••••••••••••••••• Vegan Tidbit ••••••••••••••••••

Look for unsalted chickpeas, or a brand with no added salt. This makes for the best bean-free-tasting aquafaba.

GINGERBREAD ANIMALS

As a kid, I loved celebrating Christmas by attempting old-fashioned things—making popcorn garlands, skating on our frozen pond, and, of course, baking. The cats and dogs would eat my Christmas decorations and my feet would get frozen and sore, but at least there was always baking.

This recipe is classically scrumptious holiday cheer wrapped up into a cookie: It's full of spice, lightly crisp on the outside, and soft in the middle. You can make the famous gingerbread person shape, but why not celebrate the animals at this time of year?

Prep time: 30-45 mins (including chilling time) • Cook time: 7-10 mins • Makes: About 40 cookies

DRY INGREDIENTS

3 cups all-purpose flour

1 ½ tsp baking powder

¾ tsp baking soda

¼ tsp salt

1 Tbsp ground ginger

1 Tbsp ground cinnamon

¼ tsp ground cloves

¼ tsp ground nutmeg

WET INGREDIENTS

1 Tbsp ground chia or flax seeds

2 ½ Tbsp warm water

6 Tbsp vegan butter or coconut oil, melted

¾ cup brown sugar, packed

½ cup molasses

2 tsp vanilla extract

1. Preheat your oven to 375°F. Line a baking sheet with parchment paper.

2. In a large bowl, mix together all the dry ingredients.

3. In a small bowl, mix the chia seeds into the water.

4. In another bowl, mix the soaked seeds into the other wet ingredients. Add the wet ingredients to the dry ingredients and mix just until a dough is formed. I have found that sometimes the moisture levels in vegan butters are different, so if your dough does not come together, add up to 1 Tbsp water until the dough just comes together.

5. Put the dough between two sheets of waxed paper or parchment paper and roll it out to about ¼ inch thick. Now pop it onto a baking sheet and chill the rolled dough in the freezer for 15 minutes or in the fridge for 30 minutes. Once it's chilled, cut out cookie shapes and lay them on the prepared baking sheet. Reroll the remaining dough until it's all used up, chilling in between if needed.

RECIPE CONTINUES

•••••••••• Cool Tip ••••••••••

Your average cookie recipe would call
for chilling the dough as a ball, which
requires a long chilling time and then
the dough can be difficult to roll out
as it is firm and cracks easily.
My sneaky-deaky trick in this recipe
is to roll the dough first, while it's
warm and pliable, and then chill it as a
flat sheet of dough. Chilling it allows
it to hold together well, so when
the cookies are cut and baked,
they retain their awesome
cookie-cutter shapes.

6. Bake for 7–10 minutes, then let cool completely before using Decorative Cookie Icing (below).

•••••••••••••••••• Vegan Tidbit ••••••••••••••••••

I add this because I was asked about it constantly: Eating animal-shaped cookies is totally vegan! People eat gingerbread men all the time, but that doesn't make them cannibals, right? Haha.

DECORATIVE COOKIE ICING

A simple icing that's perfect for decorating gingerbread cookies. Feel free to divide the icing once mixed, and then add different food colors to make multiple icing colors.

Prep time: 5 mins • Makes: 1 cup

1 cup icing sugar

2–4 tsp non-diary milk or water

A few drops of vegan food coloring (optional)

1. Mix the icing sugar, food coloring if using, and 2 tsp of the non-dairy milk or water. Add more non-dairy milk or water until desired consistency is reached.

CHOCOLATE-COVERED EVERYTHING CANDIES

Chocolate-covered everything! One of my favorite sweet treats is chocolate-covered raisins. Most store-bought versions contain dairy, though, so I knew I had to make my own. Not only is it SO easy to chocolate-coat raisins, you can coat any treat in chocolate—nuts, pretzels, or other dried fruit.

Prep time: 15 mins to set • Cook time: 5 mins • Makes: About 2 cups

1 cup vegan chocolate chips

1 ½ cups of any kind of nut and/or dried fruit you like (peanuts, almonds, smoked almonds, roasted cashews, walnuts, raisins, dried cranberries . . . I also like pretzels!

1. Line a baking sheet with parchment paper or a silicone mat.

2. Melt the chocolate chips in a double boiler. Once they've melted, stir in the nuts and/or dried fruit. Toss so that everything is completely coated in the chocolate.

3. Use a fork in each hand, one for scooping up the nuts and fruit and the other to help separate everything. Drop the chocolate-covered treats on the prepared baking sheet, separating them as much as possible. If you like, follow this by sprinkling on some of the optional additions (see below). Pop the sheet in the fridge for 20 minutes or freezer for 10 minutes to help set quicker. Once set, the chocolate can be stored in an airtight container at room temperature for up to a month (not that they will last that long).

• • • • • • • • • • • • • • • Amper-Uppers • • • • • • • • • • • • • • •

I had a little light bulb moment while making these. To make them extra fancy, sprinkle some bonus seasonings over the chocolate before it sets. Salted chocolate-covered raisins? Yes, please!

Salt, cinnamon, chili powder, sesame seeds, sugar, crushed candy canes, sprinkles, coconut, crushed cookies. . . . All make great add-ons. Sprinkle away, my friends.

YES, THIS REALLY IS VEGAN CHEESECAKE

Many vegan cheesecakes need to be eaten frozen. I don't like that. Cheesecake (in my mind) isn't a frozen treat. So, I was on a mission to make a bake-able vegan cheesecake that is just like the classic recipe. I realize you might be hesitant to believe that a cake made of tofu and cashews tastes just like traditional cheesecake, but I don't use the word "cheesecake" lightly. Rest assured that this cake is just as cheesy, creamy, and glorious as you would hope. Just don't tell anyone what's in it and they'll never know.

 GLUTEN-FREE

Prep time: 15 mins (+ 2 hours soaking, if required + at least 4 hours to cool + 5 mins for heavy cream) • Cook time: 48-58 mins • Makes: 1 (8-inch) cheesecake (serves 6-8)

FOR THE GRAHAM CRACKER CRUST

1 ½ cups vegan graham cracker crumbs (see Vegan Tidbit) (gluten-free, if preferred)

¼ cup vegan butter or coconut oil, melted

FOR THE CHEESECAKE FILLING

1 ½ cups raw cashews, softened (page 13)

1 cup silken tofu

½ cup Heavenly Heavy Cream (page 206) or full-fat coconut milk

½ cup white sugar

1 Tbsp cornstarch

Zest of 1 lemon, about 1 tsp

1 ½ Tbsp fresh lemon juice

2 tsp apple cider vinegar

1 tsp vanilla extract

¼ tsp salt

1. Preheat your oven to 350°F. Cut a circle of parchment paper to line the bottom of an 8-inch round baking pan.

2. For the graham cracker crust, in a medium bowl, mix the graham cracker crumbs with the melted vegan butter. Pour the mixture into the prepared pan, then press down firmly. Bake for 8 minutes.

3. In a blender or food processor, blend all the filling ingredients, including the cashews, until completely smooth. Pour over top of the graham cracker crust.

4. Return to the oven and bake for 35–40 minutes, until the edges look dry, and might even have cracked, and the center looks a little wet still but isn't liquid. The cake will be puffy but will fall as it cools. Let rest at room temperature before cooling in the fridge, uncovered, for about 4 hours or overnight.

• • • • • • • • • • • • • • Vegan Tidbit • • • • • • • • • • • • • •

Some graham crackers contain milk or honey and therefore aren't vegan. I have found brands that are vegan in the grocery store, but if you can't find vegan graham crackers, feel free to substitute any dry hard cookie that you like. Try using vanilla or chocolate wafers, or homemade Gingerbread Animals (page 191).

AH-MAZ-ING PEANUT BUTTER COOKIES

"OMG, these peanut butter cookies are ah-MAZ-ing! You need to give me the recipe immediately!"

Do you like the sound of those words? Good, because they're exactly what you'll hear every time you make this recipe. These aren't just any peanut butter cookies, these are lightly crisp on the outside, perfectly chewy in the middle, melt-in-your-mouth-sensation cookies.

Prep time: 10 mins • Cook time: 9-11 mins • Makes: About 16 large cookies

DRY INGREDIENTS

1 ¼ cups all-purpose flour

¾ tsp baking soda

¼ tsp salt

WET INGREDIENTS

½ cup natural peanut butter (smooth or crunchy)

½ cup white sugar

½ cup brown sugar, packed

½ cup vegan butter

2 tsp vanilla extract

1. Preheat your oven to 375°F. Lightly grease a baking sheet.

2. Mix all the dry ingredients together in a large bowl.

3. In a medium bowl, beat all the wet ingredients together until creamy. Add the wet ingredients to the dry ingredients and mix until just combined.

4. Using 2 Tbsp dough per cookie, roll the dough into balls and space them out on the baking sheet. Flatten each with a fork, making a crisscross pattern. Bake for 9–11 minutes, until golden.

VEGAN STAPLES

These days it's pretty easy to find many vegan staples, like eggless mayonnaise, soy sour cream, and even a few cheeses, right in your local grocery store. It really is getting easier and more convenient to be vegan. Woot woot! But sometimes it can be easier, tastier, more affordable, and definitely healthier to make your own versions at home.

LIFE-CHANGING MOZZARELLA

When I first went vegan, I quickly realized that melty, stretchy cheese is a rare find in the vegan world. Vegans need melty, stretchy, gooey pizza, too! Look no further, my vegan cheese-loving friends. This recipe will change your life.

Green olive brine or sauerkraut add a unique fermented flavor to this recipe, making it taste more like traditional cheese. I couldn't choose which flavor I preferred between the two, so I recommend trying both options to see which one you like the most.

Prep time: 5 mins • Cook time: 7 mins • Makes: About 1 ½ cups

1 cup water, plus ⅓ cup extra when called for in pizza or lasagna recipes

½ cup raw cashews, softened (see page 13)

3 Tbsp plus 1 tsp tapioca starch

2 Tbsp nutritional yeast

2 Tbsp green olive brine (the liquid in a jar of green olives) or 1 Tbsp sauerkraut

½ tsp garlic powder

½ tsp salt

1. Place all of the ingredients in your blender, and blend until completely smooth. It will be very watery.

2. Pour the mixture into a small saucepan. Stirring constantly, cook over medium heat. It will start to form clumps, and then it will all come together and turn into a cheesy goo. This will take about 5 minutes. Keep stirring and cooking for an additional minute to make sure the tapioca starch is cooked. The mozzarella is now ready to use as is, in all its melty glory.

3. Store mozzarella in an airtight container in the fridge. It will stay in a gooey state, even when chilled, and you can reheat it to melty perfection in a pot over low heat, adding a bit of water as needed to thin.

•••••••••• Cool Tip ••••••••

If you don't have a high-powered blender, you might want to pour the mixture through a fine-mesh strainer before cooking to ensure a smooth cheese consistency.

Cashews are my preference for this recipe as they provide the best texture and flavor, but if you prefer, you can sub ½ cup softened blanched almonds or softened macadamia nuts.

••••••••••••••••••• Vegan Tidbit •••••••••••••••••

A key ingredient in this recipe is tapioca starch (also called tapioca flour). It's what gives the cheese its stretch. If you use any other kind of starch it will become a thick sauce, but it will never have the same stretch, so make sure to pick up some tapioca starch. My regular grocery store sells it. If you can only find tapioca pearls, just grind those into a powder in a coffee grinder for the exact same thing!

NACHO CHEESE LOVE

There is a pretty clear reason I call this Cheese Love: This recipe is so cheesy and scrumptious it's kind of ridiculous, and you will fall in love! Just as with the Life-Changing Mozzarella (page 200), tapioca starch is the secret to making this nacho cheese the right texture—and perfect for a giant plate of nachos.

Prep time: 5 mins • Cook time: 7 mins • Makes: About 1 ½ cups

½ cup raw cashews, softened (see page 13)

1 cup water

¼ cup nutritional yeast

3 Tbsp plus 1 tsp tapioca starch

2 Tbsp green olive brine (the liquid in a jar of green olives) or 1 Tbsp sauerkraut

2 tsp fresh lemon juice

1 tsp maple syrup or agave

1 tsp regular paprika

½ tsp salt

½ tsp onion powder

½ tsp ground turmeric

¼ tsp garlic powder

1. Place all of the ingredients in your blender, and blend until completely smooth. It will be very watery.

2. Pour the mixture into a small saucepan. Stirring constantly, cook over medium heat. It will start to form clumps, and then it will all come together and turn into a cheesy goo. This will take about 5 minutes. Keep stirring and cooking for an additional minute to make sure the tapioca starch is cooked. The nacho cheese is now ready to serve, all hot and melty delicious.

3. Store leftovers in an airtight container in the fridge. Even when chilled it will stay soft. If you want to reheat, put it in a pot over low heat, adding a bit of water as needed to thin.

• • • • • • • • • • • • • • • • •   Cool Tip   • • • • • • • • • • • • • • • • •

If you don't have a high-powered blender, you might want to pour the mixture through a fine-mesh strainer before cooking to ensure a smooth cheese consistency.

Cashews are my preference as they provide the best texture and flavor, but if you prefer, you can sub ½ cup softened blanched almonds or macadamia nuts.

• • • • • • •   Amper-Uppers   • • • • • • •

For a smoked nacho cheese, use smoked paprika instead of regular paprika.

FETA FANTASTIC

This feta is perfect for Greek salads or for crumbling over pasta. Marinating tofu cubes in lemon juice breaks the tofu down so it actually gets a crumbly texture similar to traditional feta! Who knew, right? Well, I did. . . . But now you do, too!

Prep time: 15 mins to 1 hour to press + overnight to marinate
Makes: About 1 cup

3 Tbsp fresh lemon juice

1 Tbsp white miso paste

1 Tbsp olive oil

1 ½ tsp nutritional yeast

1 ½ tsp dried oregano

¼ tsp salt

½ block (6 oz) extra-firm tofu, pressed (see page 10)

1. Whisk together all of the wet ingredients to make a marinade.

2. Once the tofu is pressed, cut it into ½-inch cubes and put them in an airtight container. Pour the marinade over top and give the tofu a shake or stir to evenly coat it. Let it marinate in the fridge overnight, giving it a shake or stir every now and then. It'll keep for about a week in the fridge, and it gets even crumblier and creamier the longer it marinates.

HOW TO USE FUSS-FREE
VEGAN CHEESE

MOZZARELLA
Spread or dollop on pizza
Layer into lasagna
Make fondue
Toss into pasta
Make ooey gooey dips
Smear onto garlic bread

MACHO NACHO
Use as a dip
Drizzle over chips for nachos
Pour onto cooked broccoli
Spread on top of a veggie burger
Smother a baked potato
Make a grilled cheese

RICOTTA
Serve with spicy jelly & crackers
Use as a sandwich spread
Dollop onto hot pasta
Make it sweet and pair with fruit

FETA FANTASTIC
Make a Greek Salad
Crumble over roasted potatoes
Serve with olives & crackers
Toss into pasta
Add to any salad

PARMEGAN

This vegan parmesan is one of the very first recipes I developed, as spaghetti just isn't spaghetti without a sprinkling of cheesy goodness. Parmegan was born, and parmegan it has remained. It's still an absolute staple in my kitchen—you'll always find a big jar of it floating around somewhere. Even my omnivore parents are in love with it and make it all the time. It has a wonderful nutty, creamy saltiness that works just brilliantly on top of pasta, salad, soup, or anywhere and everywhere! I even love it sprinkled on popcorn with some finely chopped rosemary. Yeah, you should try it immediately.

 30 minutes or less · **Less than 10** ingredients · **SUPER SIMPLE** · **GLUTEN-FREE**

Prep time: 5 mins • Makes: About 1 cup

½ cup nutritional yeast

⅓ cup cashews
(raw or roasted)

⅓ cup macadamia
nuts

½ tsp salt

1. Place all the ingredients in a food processor and blend until you reach the desired texture. I like a rough sand texture, but if a fine powder is more your thing, just blend for a little longer, being careful not to blend too much or it will begin to turn into nut butter. This will keep in an airtight jar on the counter or in the fridge for up to a month.

RICOTTA I LIKE A LOT-A

I love this ricotta and use it in a number of different dishes: Tossed with pasta, thickly spread on toast and topped with sliced tomato and fresh basil, or even just with some crackers and a spicy jelly. And you know what? I've served this creamy, flavorful, elegant ricotta to some of my more food-snobby friends (no judgments!), and not only did they love it, but they also hardly believed it was vegan. I love how elegant this tastes, for how simple it really is.

Prep time: 5 mins • Makes: About 1 ½ cups

1 ½ cups raw cashews, softened (see page 13)

Zest of 1 lemon (about 1 tsp)

3 Tbsp fresh lemon juice

1 Tbsp nutritional yeast

1 tsp white miso paste

1 clove garlic

¼ cup non-dairy milk (such as soy or almond)

¼ cup water (use as needed to reach desired consistency)

1. Toss all of the ingredients in a food processor and blend it all up, stopping to scrape down the sides every now and then, until you reach a ricotta-like texture. Store in an airtight container in the fridge for up to a week.

• • • • • • • • • • • • • • •   Cool Tip   • • • • • • • • • • • • • • •

Cashews are bomb diggity in this recipe, but if they aren't your thang, you can sub blanched almonds or macadamia nuts instead. Omit the miso and garlic and add 1 tsp agave or maple syrup if you want to use this ricotta in sweet dishes, like topped on pancakes with some sliced strawberries.

HEAVENLY HEAVY CREAM

Many stores sell soy cream, almond cream, or coconut cream (often with pictures of coffee on the front), but it's really so easy to make your own cream at home with just cashews and water. My version is so luxuriously creamy—it's great in coffee, savory dishes, and sweet dishes.

Prep time: 5 mins • Makes: About 2 cups

1 cup raw cashews, softened if you don't have a high-speed blender (see page 13)

1 cup water

1. Toss the cashews and water in a blender and blend until completely smooth and creamy. Store in an airtight container or jar in the fridge for up to a week.

•••••• Amper-Uppers ••••••

To make a sweet cream, add 2 tsp maple syrup or agave (or to taste). To make vanilla cream, add ½ tsp vanilla extract.

SOUR CREAM OF MY DREAMS

I came up with this recipe on a whim, while I was waiting for my book club to arrive, as a nice complement to the chili that was bubbling on the stove. And a nice complement it was! My book club friends swarmed the cashew sour cream, scooping big spoonfuls at a time, and polished off the entire thing before the chili was even close to gone. It's the perfect way to add a bit of creaminess to a dish, and has since become a staple topping in my kitchen (and is often ~~requested~~ demanded at book club)!

Prep time: 5 mins • Makes: About 1 ½ cups

1 cup raw cashews, softened (see page 13)

½ cup water

1 Tbsp apple cider vinegar

1 Tbsp fresh lemon juice

½ tsp salt

1. Put all the ingredients in a blender and blend well, scraping the sides of the blender as needed, until very smooth and creamy. This will keep in an airtight container in the fridge for up to a week.

• • • • • • • • • • • • • • • Cool Tip • • • • • • • • • • • • • • •

Cashews are my favorite for this, as they are in some of the other recipes in this book, but you can sub 1 cup blanched almonds or macadamia nuts, if you prefer.

MAYONNAISE FOR DAYS

These days, many stores carry vegan mayonnaise, but it's easy to quickly make your own, so I say, why not? This mayo is creamy, zesty, and gorgeously thick. My trick is to use soy milk. For whatever science-y reason, I have found that only soy milk will emulsify the mayonnaise to the perfect mayo-y consistency; anything else and you'll be left with a liquid mess. Spread this thick on a sandwich, burger, or use in a salad dressing for insta-creaminess.

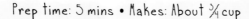

Prep time: 5 mins • Makes: About ¾ cup

¼ cup soy milk

2 tsp apple cider vinegar

1 tsp maple syrup or agave

1 tsp dried mustard

½ tsp black salt or sea salt

½ cup canola oil

1. Combine the soy milk, vinegar, maple syrup, mustard, and salt using a standing blender or an immersion blender.

2. While the blender is running, very slowly drizzle in the canola oil and a thick creamy mayo will appear before your very eyes! Store in an airtight container in the fridge for up to 2 weeks.

• • • • • • • • • • • • • • • Amper-Uppers • • • • • • • • • • • • • • •

To make an aioli, simply add 1 clove garlic along with the vinegar, then substitute the canola oil with olive oil. This is perfect with roasted potatoes, steamed artichokes, or grilled veggies of any kind.

EASIEST GRAVY IN THE WORLD

This rich, flavorful, totally luscious gravy is ideal for any holiday meal, or, you know, Tuesday. But my favorite part is that it's so easy to whip up, it takes just 5 minutes!

Cook time: 5 mins • Makes: About 1 ½ cups

3 Tbsp vegan butter

¼ cup all-purpose flour (gluten-free, if preferred)

2 cups vegetable broth

½ tsp garlic powder

½ tsp salt

⅛ tsp black pepper

1. Add the vegan butter to a saucepan over medium heat. Once melted, sprinkle over the flour and whisk until it makes a paste. Cook for 1 minute, until fragrant.

2. Pour in the vegetable broth and whisk well. Bring to a simmer, and cook, stirring often, until desired consistency is reached, about 4 minutes. Serve while hot. This will keep in an airtight in the fridge for about a week. Warm it over medium heat until hot before serving.

MY FAVORITE BBQ SAUCE

While there are many non-vegan BBQ sauces in grocery stores, there are also many vegan versions, but isn't homemade always better? It's really easy, and I can control the flavor exactly as I like it: A little smoky, a little sweet, perfect for all my BBQ-ing needs.

Prep time: 5 mins • Makes: About 1 cup

1 cup ketchup

2 Tbsp molasses

1 Tbsp soy sauce (gluten-free, if preferred)

1 Tbsp apple cider vinegar

1 Tbsp your favorite hot sauce (or to taste)

1 tsp dried mustard

½ tsp dried thyme leaves

¼ tsp liquid smoke

1. Add everything to a small bowl and stir well. Easy-peasy. Store in an airtight container in the fridge for up to 2 weeks.

ADDICTIVE COCONUT BACON BITS

Every time I make this I end up eating almost all of it straight from the jar. It's that delicious. Sprinkle it on soup, layer it into a sandwich, or toss it on top of a salad, or anywhere you think some coconut bacon bliss is needed—which, trust me, will be everywhere.

Prep time: 5 mins • Cook time: 12-17 mins • Makes: 2 cups

3 Tbsp soy sauce (gluten-free, if preferred)

2 Tbsp maple syrup

½ tsp smoked paprika

½ tsp liquid smoke

2 cups large-flake unsweetened coconut

1. Preheat your oven to 325°F. Line a large baking sheet with parchment paper.

2. Place the soy sauce, maple syrup, paprika, and liquid smoke in a large bowl and stir to combine. Add the coconut and gently toss to coat. I find it easiest to do this with my hands. Spread the coconut flakes on the baking sheet and drizzle any remaining marinade from the bowl over top.

3. Bake for 12–17 minutes, giving it a stir every now and then, until the coconut has turned dark brown. Check on it often as it nears the end of cooking time so that it doesn't burn. It will crisp up as it cools. This will keep in an airtight container in your cupboard for up to 3 weeks.

•••••••••••••••••• Vegan Tidbit ••••••••••••••••••

Large-flake coconut can sometimes be found in your regular grocery store, but if not, health food stores carry it. You can also use unsweetened coconut shreds, but keep a very close eye on it as it will take much less time (6-10 minutes) to bake.

GO-TO PIZZA DOUGH

Good news! Pizza dough is almost always vegan. Woot woot! You can buy pre-made pizza dough at most grocery stores, but it's really easy to whip up at home and will keep in the fridge for a few days.

Prep time: 1 hour 15 mins (including rising time)
Makes: Enough dough for 2 pizzas

2 ¼ tsp or 1 packet active dry yeast

1 cup warm water (think bath water temperature)

1 Tbsp maple syrup, agave, or white sugar

2 ½ cups all-purpose flour

1 Tbsp olive oil, plus more for greasing the bowl)

1 ½ tsp salt

1. Place the yeast in a large bowl with the water and maple syrup. Set aside for 10 minutes, until the mixture is foamy.

2. Mix in the flour, oil, and salt. When a dough forms, remove from the bowl and knead it for about 5 minutes on a lightly floured surface.

3. Lightly grease a clean large bowl, drop in your dough, and cover with a clean tea towel. Let rise somewhere warm for about an hour. Your oven with just the light turned on is a perfect place.

4. Once the dough has risen, it should be about doubled in size. Punch down, divide the dough into two, and knead a little bit more to form two nice balls. Use right away, or store in a plastic bag in the fridge for a few days, or freeze sealed tightly in a plastic bag and thaw before using.

• • • • • • • • • Cool Tip • • • • • • • • •

For a more nutritious dough, replace 1 cup of the all-purpose flour with 1 cup whole wheat flour.

• • • • • • • • • • • • • • • • • • • Vegan Tidbit • • • • • • • • • • • • • • • • • • •

If your yeast isn't foamy-looking after 10 minutes, it's become inactive. Buy fresh yeast and try again or your pizza dough won't rise.

MACHO NACHO POPCORN SEASONING

Popcorn is hands down my most favorite snack of all time. It's light, crispy, crunchy, you can eat a giant bowl of it yourself, and the topping combos are endless. I'm currently obsessed with this cheesy topping. Put it in a shaker and just sprinkle over popcorn as desired.

Prep time: 5 mins • Makes: About ¾ cup

½ cup nutritional yeast

¼ cup raw cashews (my fave), blanched almonds, or macadamia nuts

½ tsp salt

½ tsp smoked paprika

½ tsp sweet paprika

½ tsp onion powder

½ tsp garlic powder

1. Place everything in a small bender, food processor, or coffee grinder and grind to a fine powder. Store in an airtight jar in your pantry.

•••••••••••••••• Cool Tip ••••••••••••••••

Almond flour, cashew flour, and macadamia flour are all just the nuts ground up, so if you don't have a blender strong enough to grind nuts to a fine powder, just sub the whole nuts with your nut flour of choice.

MY NANA'S PERFECT PIE CRUST

Every now and then over the last few years I've tried to make a simple vegan pie crust recipe. I tested other people's recipes, I tried experimenting with techniques and ingredient ratios, and every time I failed miserably. It would fall apart, look terrible, and become wooden when cooked. Not at all the pie crust of my dreams.

Then genius struck! By genius, I mean my Nana. My mom has used my Nana's pie crust recipe since . . . well, since I remember existing. I asked my mom to send me the recipe, and it turns out it's basically vegan except for the milk, which is a super-easy sub. I gave it a go, and hot dang, it worked perfectly! It was quick, all the tips and techniques were there, and it was easy as pie! (Yeah, I nailed that pun, you know it.)

Prep time: 15 mins • **Makes:** 1 single layer (9-inch) pie crust

1 ½ cups all-purpose flour, plus more for rolling

¼ tsp salt (omit if using vegan butter)

¼ tsp white sugar

½ cup plus 1 Tbsp cold vegetable shortening (I like non-hydrogenated) or vegan butter, cut into cubes

¼ cup cold non-dairy milk (such as soy or almond) (see Cool Tip), plus more if needed

1. Mix the flour, salt, and sugar together in a large bowl. Add the shortening and use a fork or pastry cutter to cut it into the flour until you have a crumbly texture.

2. Drizzle the non-dairy milk across the mixture and use the fork or pastry cutter to combine until it comes together and you can form a ball of dough. Do not overmix. If the dough isn't coming together, add more milk, 1 Tbsp at a time.

3. Spread a clean tea towel over your work surface and lightly sprinkle flour over it. Scoop the dough into a rough ball and put it in the center of the floured tea towel. Roll it out until you have a rough circle that is a couple inches bigger in diameter than your pie dish, to allow room for the sides and edges of the crust. Use the tea towel to help you flip the dough into the pie dish. If some pieces fall off, that's fine. Use a knife to cut off the excess pastry around the edges, and fill any holes with some of the extra pieces of dough. Pinch the edges to form a pretty crust. Your crust is now ready to use.

To pre-cook your pie crust: Only do this if the recipe requires a baked crust prior to filling it. Preheat your oven to 450°F. Pierce the crust all over with a fork. Bake the crust for 15 minutes. Turn down the heat to 400°F and continue cooking until the crust is lightly golden, just a couple more minutes.

········· Cool Tip ·········

Before you make your pastry, make sure everything is cold. Put all of your tools, your bowl, fork or pastry cutter, and rolling pin in the fridge to chill.

I've found that different shortenings can be a little softer or firmer, making the dough hold together a little differently. You might need slightly more or less milk than I've listed here.

Feel free to double, triple, or quadruple this recipe as needed.

MENU PLANS

BRUNCH

- Dreamy Tofu Scramble ... 18
- Insanely Good Rice Paper Bacon ... 26
- Overnight Cinnamon Bun French Toast Bake ... 20
- Blueberry Bliss Muffins ... 30
- Additions: Fresh fruit

SUMMER BBQ

- Supreme Spinach Artichoke Dip ... 55
- Poppin' Jalapeño Poppers ... 52
- All Hail Caesar Salad ... 77
- Boss BBQ Veggie Burgers ... 93
- Carrot Dogs Are Totally a Thing! ... 101
- Crispy Caramel Rice Squares ... 172
- Gloriously Chewy Chocolate Chip Cookies ... 161

LUNCHBOX IDEAS

- Go-To Chickpea Salad Sandwich ... 96
- Edamame & Mandarin Orange Monster Salad ... 83
- Smoky Tomato Basil Cream Soup ... 86
- Blueberry Bliss Muffins ... 30
- Super-Simple Chocolate Chip Granola Bars ... 44

HOLIDAY FEAST

- Crowd-Pleasing Jalapeño Cheese Ball ... 62
- The Ultimate 8-Layer Dip ... 66
- All Hail Caesar Salad ... 77
- Ooh Là Là Puff Pastry-Wrapped Lentil Loaf ... 148
- Easiest Gravy in the World ... 209
- Blender Pumpkin Pie ... 174
- Magical Coconut Whipped Cream ... 181
- Gingerbread Animals ... 191
- Additions: Green beans or other veggies

DATE NIGHT

- Oh Mommy Umami Lettuce Wraps ... 60
- Creamy Rosé Linguini ... 138
- Crème Brûlée (Yes, Really) ... 185

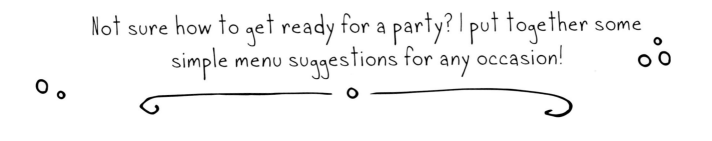

Not sure how to get ready for a party? I put together some simple menu suggestions for any occasion!

MOVIE NIGHT

- Caramelized Onion Pizza to Die For ... 137
- Popcorn with Macho Nacho Popcorn Seasoning ... 213
- Chocolate-Covered Everything Candies ... 193

DINNER PARTY

- The Ultimate 8-Layer Dip ... 66
- Crowd-Pleasing Jalapeño Cheese Ball ... 62
- Smoky Tomato Basil Cream Soup ... 86
- Very Yummy Heart of Palm Cakes ... 144
- Pumped-Up Pumpkin Penne ... 147
- Yes, This Really Is Vegan Cheesecake ... 194
- Additions: Simple side salad or some veggies

BOOK CLUB

- Oh Mommy Umami Lettuce Wraps ... 60
- Supreme Spinach Artichoke Dip ... 55
- Silky Chocolate Fudge ... 187
- Ah-maz-ing Peanut Butter Cookies ... 196

BIRTHDAY PARTY

- Pizza Dough Pretzel Bites ... 59
- Perfect Pizza Pockets ... 64
- Carrot Dogs Are Totally a Thing! ... 101
- The Best Vanilla Cake
  with Fluffy Chocolate Frosting ... 165 : 171

POTLUCK IDEAS

- The Ultimate 8-Layer Dip ... 66
- Love Letter French Onion Soup ... 80
- Very Yummy Heart of Palm Cakes ... 144
- All Hail Caesar Salad ... 77
- Lighter (: Better that Way)
  Cauliflower Fettuccini Alfredo ... 125
- Yes, This Really Is Vegan Cheesecake ... 194

CONVERSIONS & EQUIVALENTS

>>>>> MEASURMENTS <<<<<

1 tsp	→	5 ml
1 Tbsp	→	15 ml
¼ Cup	→	60 ml
⅓ Cup	→	78 ml
½ Cup	→	125 ml
1 Cup	→	250 ml

OVEN TEMPERATURES

300°F	→	150°C
325°F	→	170°C
350°F	→	180°C
375°F	→	190°C
400°F	→	200°C
425°F	→	220°C
450°F	→	230°C
475°F	→	240°C

THANK YOU

Thank you to Anne Collins for checking out my blog and sending it to Robert.

Thank you to Robert McCullough for loving my blog and inviting me in for the scariest/most fun meeting, for offering me this book deal, and for being one of the loveliest human beings ever.

Thank you to my editor, Bhavna Chauhan, for not only understanding and learning to speak my made-up words and gibberish, but becoming one of my new favorite people.

Thank you to my designer, Lisa Jager, for helping me make the most beautiful cookbook ever.

Thank you to everyone at Appetite by Random House for helping me create the cookbook of my dreams!

Thank you to my agent, Samantha Haywood, for believing in me and speaking contract on my behalf.

Thank you to my mom, Carolyn Turnbull, for ~~helping~~ doing my accounting, and for always making me a vegan option when I visit home.

Thank you to my dad, Neil Turnbull, for always pushing me to be the savvy, strong, businesswoman that I have become.

Thank you to my sister, Emma Turnbull, for always giving me the biggest, warmest hugs.

Thank you to my cousin/dear friend/ business advisor/personal trainer/recipe tester, Gretty Wilson, for letting me talk about this book to her for over 2 years straight, and still acting as interested and excited about it as I am.

Thank you to all my dear friends for being the best people in the world, giving me your honest opinions on my recipes, sharing many glasses of wine with me, and letting me yabber on obsessively about all things vegan.

Thank you to Chickpea Dog for being my snuggle buddy... if you could just learn to stop shedding, that would be great.

And lastly, thanks to YOU, my readers. Without you, none of this would have ever happened. It's the comments, emails, and photos you send me that make each and every day the best day ever.

Ok, I'll stop gushing now.

Love to all!

Bon Appetegan,

Sam Turnbull

INDEX